658.5 BLO
Blokdijk, Gerard
ITIL IT service management :

E DUE

Fri	2/12

ITIL IT Service Managem
100 Most Asked

100 Most asked questions on IT Service Man
and ITIL Foundation Certification, Training a

Gerard Blokdijk

Middleton Public Library
7425 Hubbard Avenue
Middleton, WI 53562

ITIL IT Service Management 100 Most Asked

Copyright © 2008 by Gerard Blokdijk

All rights reserved. No part of this book may be reproduced or transmitted in any form or by any means without written permission of the author.

ITIL® is a Registered Trade Mark and a Registered Community Trade Mark of the UK Office of Government Commerce (OGC). ITIL® is registered in the U.S. Patent and Trademark Office. This book and its contents are neither associated with nor endorsed by the OGC or any OGC-affiliated organization.

ITIL IT Service Management 100 Most Asked
- Gerard Blokdijk -

There has never been a ITIL IT Service Management manual like this.

100 Most Asked is *not* about the ins and outs of ITIL IT Service Management. Instead, it answers the top 100 questions that we are asked and those we come across in forums, our consultancy and education programs. It tells you exactly how to deal with those questions, with tips that have never before been offered in print.

This book is also *not* about ITIL IT Service Management's best practice and standards details. Instead, it introduces everything you want to know to be successful with and in a ITIL IT Service Management role and environment.

Table of Contents

Change Management on ITIL: Working for Changes Within the Organization

Change is something that can bring either positive or negative effect to your business or organization as a whole. Positive changes are those that are favorable, which result from careful efforts and wise decision-making, and that lead to a project's success.

Negative changes, on the other hand, are undesirable. They could be due to a lack of team effort, or misunderstandings in carrying out a particular task. Though it has often said that such unfortunate things that may occur can be analyzed and learned from so that they won't happen in the future; still, resources have been used and a lot of time and effort wasted. So, how can you be assured that positive changes will dominate your organization? The answer is Change Management.

A lot of Change Management procedures have been adapted over the years. The goal of Change Management is to make certain that systematic procedures and methods are being used to efficiently handle changes, minimizing the impact of change-related incidents and improving the day-to-day operations within the organization. Minimal disruption of services, economic utilization involved in the change and reduction in back-out activities are the main aims of Change Management.

The key activities to support the main aims of Change Management are the following:
- accept changes
- prioritize and classify changes

- coordinate change impact assessment
- coordinate approval of changes
- coordinate scheduling of changes
- coordinate implementation of changes
- conduct post implementation reviews; and
- provide management information about Change Management quality and operations.

The Role of Change Management Ticketing in ITIL

Change management is a process deliberately carried out by organizations so that they will succeed in making immense changes. When the organization is able to manage changes in a positive manner, this makes positive waves within the organization that will help it reach its objectives. The ability of the organization to handle these planned changes will affect every employee.

Implementation of the change management methods can be very disruptive to the daily activities of the organization. Discipline is required for standard operating procedures and methods to be applied well, which in turn assures prompt and well-organized handling of requests for change (commonly called RFCs). Discipline can reduce the impact of all change-related incidents as far as quality delivery of service is concerned.

Problems incurred within management of change:

Downtime can be the result, when a service provided by IT personnel is affected by change management. This causes a big problem, yet changes are often necessary so that the business can improve on and perhaps increase the number of services that it provides. These processes are usually needed because future changes have to be controlled; particularly those changes that are newly introduced to the IT environment - to minimize disturbance to the service functions and capabilities.

When change management is being instituted, there is a remarkable focus on the accomplishment of system pre-recording and tracking of RFCs. These are accomplished with the use of a simple web-based database, or help desk ticketing application. The challenges start with the identification of unmanaged and high-risk changes that are to be conveyed under the control of the CAB (Change Advisory Board.) This technology is needed to ensure that the change management procedure is not circumvented and will give the administrators the exact level of access to accomplish their given work. At the same time, limits are imposed for regulating internal policies.

Configuration Management Database (CMDB) ITIL's Standardized Database Scheme

In a modern day institution, the employer usually has a database of all its employees, each profile containing individual contact information, employment data and other credentials. Having such tool will help departments within the organization have a consistent manner of locating, and updating employee records, if ever the need arises. This does not only promote data integrity, but also, it will eliminate redundancy because a centralized employee database will only be maintained and updated by a single department, usually Human Resources. Such an information system will make it easier to produce employment certificates, as a result of employee resignation; or create employee assessment forms for possible promotion within the organization.

This concept is also similar to the Configuration Management Database or CMDB.

The CMDB stemmed from Information Technology Infrastructure Library (ITIL), and it's a repository of information connected to all the components of an information system. Its framework has always been an indispensable part of ITIL Configuration Management best practices. CMDB is a standardized database scheme intended to be used in support of an ITIL resource management project.

ITIL has a number of goals for Configuration Management, consists essentially of these four tasks:

(a)   Identification: specifies all IT assets and configurations within the organization and their inclusion in the CMDB.

(b)   Control: provide accurate information on each configuration item, specifying who is authorized to change it.

(c)   Status: records the status of all configuration items in the CMDB.

(d)   Verification: involves reviews and audits to ensure that the information contained in the CMDB is accurate, and correct of any exceptions, if necessary.

The Steps Involved in Using CMMI ITIL

Capability Maturity Model Integration (or CMMI) is a process of improvement used by organizations, which encompasses elements that are essential and effective to organizational functions. CMMI can be used to guide improvements of processes within projects, subdivisions, or even an entire organization. It aids in integrating traditional and independent organizational functions to allow for guidance in quality processes, sets in place a process to improve priorities and goals, and offers points of reference necessary for appraisal of current processes.

Getting started with CMMI

The first step involves securing appropriate sponsorship and funding. Before you even try out a process improvement effort, try to ensure that you have enough funds to sponsor the program management initiative. Sponsoring and funding are critical to ensure its success.

Second, you must understand the basic concepts of the CMMI process. Attend to its introductory courses, and also pursue training, if doable.

Next, take steps to prepare your organization for the changes. Treating process improvement as a company project will help the changes proceed smoothly.

Try to establish the business goals and objectives to heighten efforts at improvement. Discuss perceived effects, benefits and costs with the people concerned, to allow for a persuasive presentation of the opportunities and problems that may arise.

Form an engineering process group that will coordinate the sequence of activities within the enterprise. Members of this group may serve as mentors for others throughout the improvement process.

The fifth step involves knowing your stand; mapping CMMI for analysis to determine the process of your organization; and comparing it with CMMI models as part of the appraisal method. Gather data from managers, project leaders, and workers by surveying. This results in identification of the opportunities and elimination of the barriers to changes.

Communicate and coordinate with everyone. Be honest and be open when communicating by listening to the comments and suggestions of others.

In conclusion, CMMI will necessitate tracking your progress. Compare where your organization stands right now, and then look at where you want to go. This helps you to focus on your progress throughout the improvement program.

A Short Description of ITIL History- The Best Way to Define ITIL

Information Technology (IT) is now considered a way of life. Through the years, IT has established its importance not only in the field of education and other industries, but more significantly in the world of business. It has made things easier for companies to accomplish business needs and goals, and carry out operational tasks. Because of the rapidly growing dependency of many business firms to Information Technology, the United Kingdom's Central Computer and Telecommunications Agency (CCTA) has sought the essence of developing a set of standards for achieving quality service, and at the same time, overcoming difficulties linked to the growth of IT systems. Hence, the Information Technology Infrastructure Library (ITIL) was introduced to the world, and has become the de facto standard in IT service management.

Now currently maintained and developed by the Office of Government Commerce, ITIL has been adopted and adapted by almost every type of IT environment. ITIL is a set of best practices and guidelines that define a systematic and specialized approach to the management of IT service provision. These guiding principles are intended to promote value of IT operations by delivering high quality services.

Implementing this extensive set of management procedures will lead to benefits such as:

(a)   Get more out of existing resources, resulting in reduced costs;

(b)   Improved customer satisfaction through a more proficient approach to IT service delivery;

(c)   Improved productivity by eliminating redundant work;

(d) Improved service quality though the use of established best practice processes;

(e) Improved use of skills and experience, defining a consistent level of service.

How to Employ ITIL Principles to Improve Your IT Organization

When it comes to the metrics and standards of business process, does your IT company have guidelines to follow? If the answer to this question is no, then it is high time for you to think of getting your managers and IT department heads ITIL certified. For years now, Information Technology Infrastructure Library or ITIL has set the bar high for IT companies around the world with the 'best practices' guidelines and frameworks they have. If you want to be able to compete in the global market, and offer the highest quality of IT services to your clients, then ITIL implementation is a must.

First, take a look at the benefits of ITIL. With this, you can save on your operational costs, and save a lot of time and effort in improving the business processes implemented within your organization. Another benefit is that the time-tested processes used in ITIL will definitely boost the quality of the IT services that your company delivers to its customers. As a result, the higher your quality of service, the higher the customer satisfaction rate is.

Within the walls of the company itself, you will see increased productivity, and you can also maximize your manpower. More importantly, the standards used in the implementation of ITIL business processes will put your business up to par with the rest of the world. With all these benefits and more, there is absolutely no reason for you to not use ITIL to enhance the IT services that you offer to your clients. Which, at the end of the day, will also improve your day-to-day operations.

Discover the New ITIL Version 3

The growing demand on the use of ITIL led to the upgrade from ITIL version 2 to ITIL version 3. Version 2 was focused on the processes, particularly on the operational processes. The version 3 upgrade was set to focus on service management practice guidance. As a minor side note, one of the upgrades 3 was that "The IT Infrastructure Library" was changed to "ITIL Service Management Practices". The name change implied the ITIL's evolution to a broader scope; a holistic approach in the style of IT service management, one that is value-based and business focused. The ITIL version 3 consists of a set of core texts supported with complementary and web-based materials. While ITIL version 2 volumes where available only in English, version 3 was made available in other languages.

ITIL v3 core volumes include service strategy, service design, service transition, operation services, and continual service improvement. The word "continual" was used for the ITIL version 3 instead of the word "continuous" as used in version 2. The word continual was believed to be better suited to define activities intended to function without pause, as the goal of service management is "availability."

Other extras from ITIL version 3 include:
An extra volume, considered a core volume, titled "The Official Introduction to the ITIL Service Lifecycle" by Sharon Taylor, Chief Architect for ITIL V3 (ISBN-10: 0113310617).
A complimentary material that shows the major changes in the way businesses procure and utilize their IT services. It includes process maps and governance mapping and other frameworks (e.g. COBIT) and methodologies (e.g. Six Sigma).

ITIL v3 web-based material tends to support more recent updates, and allow wider breadth of coverage of ITIL guidance through case studies.

ITIL Capacity Management

Realizing the importance of cost-effective project implementation, the ITIL Capacity Management process ensures that provisions of IT services are at their optimum and cost-effective level by helping IT companies match their available resources to the demands of the business. It is a key element for proactive engineering of IT services, making sure that certain IT resources and infrastructure can be utilized or are made available should the need arises. Capacity Management activities include the following:

- Monitoring and modeling to simulate the performance of IT services and its supporting components, and understand future resource needs.
- Analyzing, tuning, and implementing necessary activities to make efficient uses and changes in resource utilization.
- Managing and understanding the current demands for computing resources and deriving forecasts for future requirements, which involves an understanding of business priorities.
- Application sizing to ensure required service levels can be met.
- Building the yearly infrastructure growth plan with input from other team members.
- Storing capacity management data while predicting the IT resources needed to achieve agreed service levels.
- Producing a capacity plan that documents current utilization and forecasted requirements, as well as support costs for new applications or releases.

In addition, one of the main reasons why ITIL Capacity Management should be implemented first is that it offers fast and early wins that will often produce enough cost savings to finance the remainder of the ITIL project. Demonstrating success and recovering implementation costs early on also helps encourage management to stay intact, and gain momentum for the project while easing out organizational resistance. These definite advantages make ITIL Capacity Management a good candidate for a pilot implementation of the project.

ITIL CMM and Six Sigma: Three for the Company

Competition among companies nowadays has become more and more IT oriented. We now have an assortment of quality standards that have improved business processes. ISO9000, Six Sigma, Capability Maturity Model (CMM), Information Technology Infrastructure Library (ITIL) are just a few of them. While these quality programs may have overlapping concepts and processes, they actually all work together to provide a better quality of service. They all have their strengths and limitations, so a combination of them may be availed from the organization. ITIL, CMM and Six Sigma combined can be beneficial to the organization because they work hand in hand in addressing the limitations of the one another.

ITIL was first started in the UK Office of Government Commerce to provide IT service management best practices. This is a detailed and IT-focused training where operational issues are greatly analyzed and addressed, and future needs of the IT business are always taken into consideration.

Since ITIL is mainly operational in nature (how-to), this is its main limitation, and this is where the strength of CMM comes in. CMM was developed by the Carnegie Mellon University Software Engineering Institute. Now called the Capability Maturity Model Integration or CMMI, it focuses mainly on what the company needs to do in order to change its status from a state of no-order to a precision-based, error- free IT organization.

Six Sigma was developed by Motorola Inc., as a means of measuring service from a customer's perspective. Its main objective is to create a service or product that is free from defects the first time it is released. By doing this, companies eliminate the problems faced by most other companies where defects are seen after the release of the product or service. Since it was developed by Motorola, the design of Six Sigma was for the manufacturing industry and there are limitations when it comes to IT software development (like beta-testing and debugging).

The process of Six Sigma's make-it-right-the-first-time, combined with CMM's what- to-do, and ITIL's how-to-do-it makes ITIL and CMM and Six Sigma a powerful combination training tool for the organization. After all, quality products and services are still virtues any organization should have.

The Importance of ITIL Process Map and What it Can Do to Your Business

ITIL has a Process Map that offers ITIL contents in clear and graphical structure. The ITIL is actually designed to assist you in planning and taking necessary steps in ITIL. Working with the best practice principles in your company, using it will give you great advantages in the industry: Benefits of ITIL process map are:

By using an easy to navigate and graphical structure, this can assist in the awareness of the complex processes and ITIL procedures.

The variety of processes and performing complimentary projects gives appropriate guidance on how to arrange implementation projects.

You can save energy and effort in the process of documentation and designing while you are adapting current process models and document outlines. This is much better than starting from scratch.

In following this process map, you can be assured of high quality documentation. This is a very important tool to promote your IT organization, to be competent, and to be an effective source of IT services. The best technique in creating a Process Map is to utilize easy flowcharting software. There are steps in Process Mapping that consists of the following:

a) Identification of process: This is to reach a full understanding of procedures and processes.

b) Gathering information: It is vital in process mapping that you recognize the objectives, key controls and other risks that may take place.

c) Mapping and interviewing: it is important that you understand the ideas in designing and processing the maps.

d)   Analysis: This will help you develop tools and methods to create the process in an efficient and effective manner. Information Technology Infrastructure Library Process Map is an efficient tool in improving your IT processes. It is also significant that you find ways to improve, develop and upgrade your system to effectively manage your IT service for your clients.

Reasons Why You Need ITIL Capacity Management

ITIL Capacity Management is actually just one of the five elements of the ITIL Service Delivery area. It is responsible for guaranteeing the business requirements, and service definitions are accomplished by utilizing the least amount of computing resources.

Capacity Management consists of a number of activities. They are:

- This process includes observing, modifying, evaluating and implementing necessary changes in resource consumption.
- It is imperative to manage the requests for computing resources, that requires knowledge, and understanding the priorities of your business.
- To encourage infrastructure performance and know upcoming resource requirements, modeling is an important process in capacity management.
- This process includes collecting capacity management data.
- To guarantee that the service levels are accomplished, sizing applications are included in capacity management.
- Procedures such as creating a capacity plan that records present consumption, support cost for latest application and anticipated requirements are to be done in capacity management.
- Brainstorming new ideas with other teams in creating an infrastructure development plan is one of the essential activities in ITIL capacity management.

Reasons why you should apply capacity management in your business are:

a. In implementing capacity management, you can get a lot of existing IT resources, and this could improve the cost of the IT service unit position.

b. By going through this process, you can also get rid of redundant work and guarantee reliable reporting.

c. This can give timely capacity and other connected cost information to have a more organized and informed business decision.

d. The process can offer a wide range of inputs to TCO. This could also provide major IT related programs and upgrades.

Information Technology Infrastructure Library (ITIL) Capacity Management works closely with ITIL Financial Management and Service Level Management. By having processes like ITIL Capacity Management, a systematic service level is linked to financial information and allows the leaders in your business to make accurate, organized and informed decisions.

The ITIL Certification Course

Companies and businesses today all want to maximize their IT operations. With so many ways to approach a given IT situation, organizations all want the most effective method, procedure, process or technique. This is known as best practice. But with information technology increasingly getting more complicated, a set of best practices has been established in what is now called the Information Technology Infrastructure Library or ITIL. And now, more and more companies are getting an ITIL certification.

Getting this certification has now become a worldwide standard for all IT service management. The basic concepts and principles established by the UK Office of Government Commerce have not changed, and will still cover service strategy, service design, service transition, service operation and continual service improvement. It will also include service support and service delivery.

Today, ITIL courses come in ITIL v2 and ITIL v3, but individuals and corporations wishing to get a complete ITIL certification still have to finish three subjects: Foundation, Practitioner and Manager. All ITIL Certification courses will begin with the basic foundation of ITIL. Definitions, terminologies, its history and basic principles will thoroughly be discussed, along with the service support and service delivery. At the end of this course, participants are expected to take the ITIL Foundation Certification exam.

Upon completion of and passing the ITIL Foundation Certification, the Practitioner's Certificate is the next step. An ITIL Change, Configuration and Release Management exam, and an ITIL Service Desk, Incident and Problem Management exam will be given in order for the student to get the ITIL Certification for Practitioner.

Experienced professionals, who have mastered the ITIL service management functions, can take the ITIL Certification for Managers or ITIL Manager's Certificate.

ITIL v3 library is the latest addition to ITIL. Published in June 2007, it encompasses the most adopted worldwide standard for best practices in IT management. And ITIL Certification for v3 is also given to individuals who have finished the courses for v2.

What is ITIL Change Management?

To guarantee an effective supply of services in Information Technology, it is very important to deal with the changes in your system. This can reduce any disturbance in delivering IT services to your customers. Change management includes elements of IT infrastructure such as documentations, hardware and software. IT service and IT service organizations are also included in Change Management. What are the functions of change management? It aims to make sure that the standard procedures and methods are implemented. This is to efficiently manage the changes in the system and reduce the amount of impact in the service quality of your company. The Change Management strategy for an organization can support the whole IT Service Management Infrastructure. It will regulate or support the victory of ITIL processes.

Change Management Workflow

The ITIL compliant management system maintains a wide range of intricate workflow selections, as follows:
- Recursive: this is an effect on the rejection in a workflow. A part of that workflow is relocated and opened.
- Concurrent multi tasking: this is a sequence of tasks that can happen all at the same time in a workflow.
- Automatic closure of used paths: this process of approval has several paths, and the system will be able to close any unused paths.
- Dependencies: the process of tasks and approvals which are reliant on other tasks. And there are approvals that are completed in advance, by simply having uncomplicated linear workflow. There are a great number of problems that threatens IT services; one being because it is a badly executed change. Instead

of trying to focus on the incident management, some people try to deal with the problem after the damage is done. And most of the IT businesses today seek change management to avoid the occurrence of these problems. If you don't enhance and improve your Change Management strategies, your company will be prone to continuous firefighting.

Understanding ITIL Concepts and Terminology

The IT Infrastructure Library (ITIL) consists of the best practices in the field of service management. Since the ITIL has been a worldwide practice, the concepts and terminologies were clearly defined so as for all IT users to understand, and make it easier for non-IT users to appreciate. The following are some of the concepts and terminologies that ITIL provides:

- Service Level Management: the process of ensuring that the Service Level Agreements (SLAs) between the company and customer are documented. It is at this level that the actual supplied service is monitored and delivered in conformance with SLAs.
- Financial Management for IT Services: the process where the company identifies the clear objective of the ITIL, which are the cost-effective ownership and handling of IT resources so as to provide IT services. The Financial Management process tends to decrease or reduce the overall long-term costs and actual costs of services provided.
- Incident Management: the process of protecting service continuity. It seeks to restore quickly normal service operation with minimal impact to business operations.
- Problem Management: the process of recording to the Configuration Management Database incidents that might give rise to a known or unknown problem.
- Configuration Management: the process of maintaining and controlling all versions of the IT Configuration. It provides accurate information that will support the service management processes. The

functions of staff, documentation, organization charts, the Definitive Software Library (DSL) and Definitive Hardware Library (DHL) for any released products are stored in the CMDB.

ITIL concepts and terminologies allow managers without IT knowledge to have a holistic view of the IT service management. The worldwide acceptance likewise changed the view of service management from operational to performance based.

General Tips in Taking an ITIL Exam

Individuals and organizations that have ITIL Certifications will surely have an edge when it comes to best practice approaches in IT operations. But in order to get an ITIL Certification, you still need to take an ITIL foundation, practitioner and service manager exam.

Getting certified in all three components of ITIL is no easy matter. So you should choose a school with a good reputation and passing statistics on ITIL exams. In getting your exams, a few practical tips should be followed.

First, get your terminologies right! Your ITIL exam, especially the foundation certificate, will contain numerous terminologies on the subject. Use them frequently and use them correctly.

Some questions will definitely require you to write an essay about ITIL. So read the questions carefully twice to make sure that you understand them. Then answer them clearly, completely, concisely and directly. Do not babble on and on about ITIL subjects that are not even relevant to the questions. Remember that examiners mark you on your correct answers and not on how long your essays are.

Since all topics, processes, methods and techniques will be covered in the ITIL exam, make sure that you have reviewed the following: benefits, advantages, limitations, disadvantages, terminologies, history and application.

As a general rule, in any exam that you take, do not linger on a particular question longer than a couple of minutes. If you think that a particular ITIL exam question is difficult to answer, skip it and come back to it later. Your target is to answer confidently (not necessarily correctly) at least 75% of the ITIL exam.

ITIL Fault Tree Analysis: Determining the Root Cause of Failures

An ITIL fault tree analysis (FTA) is used when an undesirable result of the ITIL process is determined to have occurred. It is a more complex cause-effect flow that people use to better understand, solve and prevent such potential failures from happening. In this technique, an undesired effect is taken as the root (or also called the top event) of a logic tree; then each situation or circumstance that could result from that effect is added to the tree as a series of logical expressions. The logical operator, such as an AND or OR gates, can be used to represent the series of errors and their corresponding causes.

To have a more detailed flow in coming up with an FTA, six simple steps on how to design it were cited by Hank Marquis. All you need is a pencil, a piece of paper and a working knowledge of the service. These are the steps:

1. Try to be more specific in coming up with a top-level event for your analysis. Some examples include potential or known error messages and possible scenarios that can be thought of, based on the Service Level Agreement or SLA.
2. Write down all the faults under the top level event in boxes and connect the fault boxes to the top level event box by drawing lines.
3. For each fault, list as many causes as possible.
4. Draw a diagram and use the AND and/or OR logic operators.
5. Continue identifying the causes of the problem until the root cause is identified.

6. Consider coming up with countermeasures to find ways on how to resolve such issues and learn from them.

Reasons Why You Should Take ITIL Foundation Course

The Information Technology Infrastructure Library or ITIL Foundation is the first step of any individual or organization wishing to get an ITIL certification for IT service management. The ITIL Foundation covers all the basic information and terminologies used in ITIL, including its history, growth, improvements and coverage.

The ITIL Foundation covers five core sets of IT service management concepts which include the Service Strategy, Service Design, Service Transition, Service Operation and Continual Service Management. Basically focusing on service support and service delivery, ITIL Foundation also covers ITIL v3. It is the latest addition to the IT service management library. It covers the most adopted principles and concepts of ITIL and includes the ITIL Service Lifecycle concept to IT service management.

What you will learn on ITIL Foundation:

Discovering and exploring the different ITIL principles to decrease hardware failure is one of the topics you will learn in this course. This course will get you ready for the ITIL v3 Foundation Certification Exam. You will recognize the opportunities to build IT processes by utilizing ITIL v3. Aside from that you can work together with IT teams using ITIL terminology and ideas. Through this, you will recognize the significance of IT and business integration. It is very important that you explore and discover the components of Service Management processes. By enrolling in this course you will learn and see the benefits of Continual Service Improvement in a company.

Benefits in taking this course:

This unique process and format in the course follows the guiding principles and gives broad coverage of ITIL v3 Foundation Certification Exam subjects. The Information Technology Infrastructure library (ITIL) v3 is the latest version that is used in best practice framework in IT. Attaining the Foundation Certification signifies clearly that you can play a great part in improving the IT system in your organization.

ITIL Foundation: The First Step to ITIL Success

All businesses today are highly dependent on IT. But with IT advances, some companies are finding it hard to implement a successful IT infrastructure. This is where ITIL comes in. A certification in ITIL will promise you improved efficiency, reduced risk and faster resolution of problems. This translates to better handling of resources and reduced cost. ITIL Foundation is the first step in understanding the concepts of ITIL. The ITIL Foundation will introduce you to the terminologies, philosophies, background and history of ITIL.

The ITIL Foundation is ideal for all IT managers and staff engaged in the development of service and support of their IT infrastructure. This is the beginner's level, which will give an overview to the participants, and allow them to become familiar with all best practices in ITIL. The ITIL Foundation is also ideal for people who are not directly involved in the implementation of the best practices, but are required to understand ITIL concepts and terminologies in order for them to evaluate properly IT service management.

Getting an understanding of the ITIL Foundation will enable the business to clearly classify roles and responsibilities of its IT managers and staff, resulting in a more efficient and effective organization. Since the adopted IT processes and procedures are standardized, understood, streamlined and well arranged; service delivery will be improved and businesses can focus on more consistent and reliable partnerships with its customers and users.

There are now several institutions offering ITIL Foundation trainings, seminars and workshops both online and in-house. They will give you case studies, sample exam questions, reviews and different activities in order to prepare you for the ITIL Foundation certification.

ITIL Framework: The Backbone of ITIL Functions and Processes

Information Technology Infrastructure Library (ITIL) is comprised of a series of books written for the purpose of outlining a set of management procedures to facilitate the delivery of high quality services in the field of Information Technology (IT). It is a framework of interlinking processes developed to assist with the increasing challenges linked to maintaining a more secure, compliant and stable IT organization.

The ITIL framework has turned out to be the benchmark for IT organizations. ITIL V2 consists of seven modules that constitute the core of ITIL, with the task of determining how IT can best serve the needs of the business. These are the following:

- Service Delivery: covers the processes required for the development, and planning of quality IT services and improvement of services delivered looking forward.
- Service Support: focuses on the processes associated with the day-to-day support and maintenance activities that include ensuring all users of the ICT services have access to the appropriate tools to support the business functions.
- ICT Infrastructure Management: involves processes within ITIL that are linked to ICT equipment and software.
- Planning to Implement Service Management: examines the issues and tasks involved in planning, implementing and improving Service Management processes within the organization.

- Application Management: describes how to manage applications through the life-cycle of software development projects.
- The Business Perspective: a collection of best practices and guidance to help IT personnel understand their contribution to the business objectives.
- Security Management: details the process of planning and managing a defined level of security to guarantee the safety of information.

ITIL Help Desk: How ITIL Can Help Improve Your Help Desk Services

The service/help desk is a fundamental element of IT services. Since help desks are front liners of your company, it is important that you maintain a good quality in IT services. The Help desk is your customers' fist contact that they can run to if they are having a hard time figuring out technical problems. That is why IT help desk is certainly a valuable unit in your business. With ITIL Service/help desk, the company can help improve the services that they can offer their customers. With a technology based company, it is expected that the company can handle and manage the system of service to improve the business. To aid companies in call centers and help desks, and improve their IT services, ITIL teaches organizations the value of help desks in IT services.

ITIL builds a framework to enhance and improve the quality of your services. It also helps you recognize the strengths and weaknesses of the organization's help desk. In identifying the weaknesses, the company can now develop guides to find solutions to them and overcome technical problems. The ITIL stresses best business practices and other administration strategies to improve the organization's help desk. It also gives a broad and consistent set of principles to manage IT services appropriately. It creates a setting that produces premium quality service. The ITIL concentrates on the processes, IT issues, business practices and its people.

The Information Technology Infrastructure Library has eight instruction manuals that talk about various characteristics of service management in the help desk. It is very important that guidelines are met. Technology upgrades everyday and if your help desk system does not have room to implement these improvements and upgrades, then having service management problems are to be expected.

ITIL in Action: Service Delivery

The ITIL v2 framework covers two IT Service Management Sets: ITIL Service Delivery and ITIL Service Support.

ITIL Service Delivery is a proactive approach to the business requirements of users through the proper analysis of existing infrastructure in order to predict future needs. It involves five sub processes as follows:

- Service Level Management. It will continually align the IT services with the requirements of the business, with the goal of creating and delivering a clear method of services expected versus actually services delivered.
- Capacity Management. This involves appropriately determing existing business IT infrastructure, and predicting future needs in order to avoid bottlenecks that may hinder business development.
- Financial Management for IT Service. This will define the cost of availing the current and future service needs of the organization and ensure that expenditures are with the planned budget.
- Availability Management. This assures that IT services are always online and ready when they are needed by the users and customers.
- IT Service Continuity Management. This is also known as Contingency Management, and it will provide a framework for recovering from IT disruptions caused by human or natural disasters.

With ITIL Service Delivery, users, customers and service providers can properly define the content, role and responsibilities of each party so that they can set expectations of the speed, quality and availability of the service.

ITIL Service Delivery will work upon and improve on existing IT infrastructure for continuous improvement of service. It is custom made to specifically meet the needs of businesses. ITIL Service Delivery clearly illustrates a responsible corporate behavior in the use of the IT infrastructure in order to maximize profits and reduce unnecessary expenses.

ITIL Incident Management Course: Minimizing the Adverse Effects of Incidents

Training institutions are offering a wide range of courses, covering all the processes involved in the implementation of Information Technology Infrastructure Library. One of these processes is Incident Management, wherein its goal is to restore normal service operation of the business as quickly as possible, as this is also specified in the Service Level Agreement (SLA) and minimize the adverse effects of certain incidents in the operation. Because of this, the best possible levels of service quality and availability are maintained.

Incident Management should be used to make sure that the best application of resources to support the business is in place. At the same time, it should develop and maintain meaningful records relating to certain incidents, while devising a countermeasure and applying a consistent approach to all incidents reported. Overall, Incident Management is responsible for the following:

(a) Classification of all incidents that occurred.
(b) Incident detection and recording.
(c) Initial support, investigation and analysis.
(d) Resolution and recovery.
(e) Incident closure.
(f) Incident ownership and monitoring.

There is a specific team that handles Incident Management duties, and it is called the Incident Response Team (IRT), or an Incident Management Team (IMT). They are specifically designated for the task of ensuring that hazards within the organization can be identified, analyzed and corrected. This team really plays a major role in the company's security and maintaining its operation when possible threats or unexpected incidents take over. With very challenging and stressful work, one should really take incident management courses. Having a profound knowledge of Incident Management will surely eradicate threats that may come along within the course of the ITIL project.

ITIL Incident Management Seminars: Honing Incident Troubleshooting Skills

An incident in information technology refers to any event which is not part of the standard operation of the service and which causes, or may eventually cause, a threat, interruption or reduction of the quality of service provided. It is, however, the objective of Information Technology Infrastructure Library (ITIL) Incident Management to restore the normal operations of the business as quickly as possible with the slightest possible impact on both parties, either the provider or the end user, at the most cost-effective manner.

Since Incident Management is considered one of the most essential processes of ITIL, there are a lot of ITIL Incident Management seminars. They're conducted for the purpose of sharing best practices on how to handle incidents, which may include detection, investigation and analysis of incidents that may occur in certain situations or scenarios. Input for Incident Management usually comes from the users. Such unfortunate occurrences in the IT environment include system outages, service interruptions or other external threats like bad weather conditions.

It is indeed a big help if all Incident Management personnel attend seminars that will surely hone their skills in incident troubleshooting. The Incident Management Team should realize the importance of time in resolving such incidents, which is why the Incident Management Life Cycle should be taken into consideration at all times to keep up with the demands of the business, as well as the Service Level Agreement (SLA). Therefore, the critical success factors of Incident Management are the following:

(a) Maintaining IT Service Quality;
(b) Maintaining Customer Satisfaction; and
(c) Resolving incidents within established service times.

ITIL Incident Management: Technologies for Customer Satisfaction

ITIL Incident Management aims to identify, process, resolve and restore IT services. This procedure is responsible for processing and getting Service Requests and supporting users in IT downtimes. In this process the users have regular intervals in incident status. ITIL Incident Management is part of the ITIL Support area.

The technology in Incident Management is more reactive than proactive because the process provides guidelines and procedures on already identified error incidents in order to restore them. The Incident Management is an immediate process. This procedure gives guidance on analytic procedures necessary to establish quick services.

The main focus of Incident Management is to prioritize incidents in terms of urgency and impact, detect and record the details of the event, match it with known problems in order to track down the best solution, re-establish the services needed by the user or customer, and finally to pass on details of the event to other staff for the efficient and timely resolution of the problem(s).

The goal of ITIL Incident Management Technology is to minimize the damaging effects of service disruptions through swift restoration of normal service operations in accordance with the service level agreement.

The advantages of implementing this process are sustaining service levels promised to the user/customer by means of meeting the service accessibility needs. ITIL Incident Management technology will attempt to reduce or avoid service downtimes. This improves productivity and effectiveness of your staff through proper channeling and escalation of events. This in turn will surely create satisfied and happy customers.

Benefits of Incident Management Tool

You can not afford delays in your production. You need to beat the time and date you have committed to deliver the company's product or services. Due to unavoidable instances, a problem during production may occur, and you need to account for this incident.

One of the components of ITIL Service Support is the Incident Management. It is in this process where management should be able to restore the service to normal operation following an incident. Activities involve in handling Incident management are as follows:

- To be able to detect and record incident in detail.
- To be able to match incidents versus known problems.
- To be able to resolve incidents as soon as possible.
- To be able to prioritize incidents with respect to impact and need.
- To be able to bring to the attention to other teams the incident for appropriate timely resolution.

Software is made available as a tool for handling incident management problems. The following are some of benefits that the software provides:

- It allows management to gather information as to the real time and historical data of what transpired.
- It allows identification as to the bottlenecks in terms of performance.
- It speeds up the restoration of the operation as causes of incidents can be clearly identified.

- It minimizes the recurrence of incidents by informing IT users of the impact that the incident has caused to the system.

The use of Incident Management tools within your organization will yield great benefits in terms of maintaining the service levels, meeting the service availability requirements, increasing the efficiency and productivity of staff, and most importantly improving user's satisfaction.

The Proven Tips to Pass the ITIL Input/Output Manager's Exam

Yes, it is indeed very challenging, but at the same time rewarding to fill the shoes of an ITIL manager. There are a lot of things to consider, with the main goal being to coordinate and make conscious efforts in partnership with the business to deliver high quality IT service. The main procedure of realizing this goal is the operation of effective processes by making wise use of resources available and the provision of appropriate value for cost effective services. To achieve this, the correct processes need to be in place, and at the same time developed and implemented by the right people. Delegation is indeed one of the primary duties of an ITIL manager.

Though there are a lot of challenges in store for an ITIL manager, still there are a lot of people who are interested in making it into the ITIL managers' circle. With a minimum requirement of five (5) years in a managerial position, and a working knowledge of IT processes, the Manager Certificate Course is indeed considered the highest level of all ITIL training courses. To pass the Manager exam with flying colors, here are some suggestions that one may consider:

- Treat the proctor as your client and provide logical answers as if you are in front of the client.
- Show that you are a consistent solution provider by revisiting some of the best practices you have followed with your years of experience as a manager.
- Make every question count. Answer each question in such a way that the proctor will have pleasure reading it.

- Review your answers for each question and re-read them. Skip difficult ones, and go over them when you're done with the easy ones.

ITIL Jobs: What Employees and Job-seekers Should Know

To be able to have a successful IT Service management within your company, getting the right people on the job is very important. Hiring staff in your management positions can make or break your business. As they say, the key to people management is having the best people to manage. Locating these people is not easy. And, as for jobseekers, finding the right company is a tough job as well. This includes numerous interviews that don't meet the career path you want to take. If you are a businessman looking for staff to complete your team in IT service management you can go through this list of must haves in ITIL. Most of the Information Technology Infrastructure Library jobs look for people responsible for a certain discipline in Service Support and Service Delivery. Here are some criteria that companies want:

- Since most of the time the jobs require dealing with people and customers in the service industry, the jobs in ITIL require having good interpersonal and communication skills.
- Of course, it is very important to have keen knowledge of ITIL. Management requires applicants to have certifications such as Practitioner, Foundation or Management level.
- The jobs also require having staff management and leadership skills to handle the staff/team properly.
- Knowledge in financial management, and executing the service management discipline is a must for all who aim to have a career in ITIL.
- Knowledge on the most recent technology in IT in line with the discipline is vital. Maintaining the inter-

faces and sustaining the effectiveness of the procedure is also crucial in this line of work.

These are just some of the vital job requirements in ITIL.
And if you are a jobseeker interested in the ITIL business, you
should prepare yourself, for there are a variety of opportunities for
you in this industry.

What is the meaning of "ITIL Methodology"?

Information Technology Infrastructure Library (ITIL) is basically a compilation of the best practices that are intended to improve and uphold a particular level of quality computing services in IT. This process consists of skill requirements and organizational structure for the IT organization through a very broad procedure. In ITIL V2, there are seven (7) books, and each is set up for different kinds of disciplines:

- Service Delivery: it discusses the processes necessary in planning and developing high quality IT services. This is a long term process that is connected with developing and delivering quality IT service. This includes the following: Capacity Management, IT Financial Management, Availability Management, Service Level Management and IT Continuity Management.
- Service Support: this explains the different processes that are associated with the everyday maintenance and support that is needed in IT services. This includes Release Management, Change Management, Problem Management, Incident Management, Configuration Management and Service Desk.
- Implement Service Management: This analyzes the issues and tasks that include planning, improving the service management and applying service management.
- Security Management: this is a detailed process in planning and supervising security level in IT services.

- Information and Communications Technology (ICT) Infrastructure Management: this deals with the identification of business needs and other procurement procedures. This includes Network Service Management, Systems Management, Computer Installation and acceptance, Operations Management, Management of local processors.
- The Business Perspective: this gives help and guidance to IT staff to know how they can play a role in contributing to business objectives.
- Application Management: this explains the management of applications to the initial business requirement(s). It gives emphasis in making sure that IT techniques and projects are aligned with the business. ITIL methodology is a comprehensive process that will enable IT operations to manage and organize their system and applications. This kind of procedure does not depend solely on a certain technology given by a vendor. This process applies to every feature of IT Infrastructure.

ITIL Capacity Management: Toward Providing Consistent Levels of Service

One of the processes involved in managing information technology is Capacity Management, more specially in the ITIL Service Delivery area. Capacity Management aims to understand the future requirements of the business (the required delivery of service), the IT infrastructure (the means of service delivery), and the operation of the organization (the current service delivery). While at the same time ensuring that all current and future capacity and performance aspects of the business requirements are provided at the right time in the most efficient and cost-effective manner.

Capacity Management has three main areas of responsibility. These are the following:

- Business Capacity Management (BCM): ensures that careful planning and implementation of future business requirements for IT services are delivered in a timely fashion.
- Service Capacity Management (SCM): focuses on monitoring the performance of IT services provided to consumers; and
- Resource Capacity Management (RCM): focuses on the management of IT infrastructure, while making sure that all finite resources are being measured and monitored.

There are a lot of reasons why Capacity Management should be implemented within an organization. Benefits, either long term or immediate, include reduced costs, improved service quality and more consistent levels of service. Some of the processes involved in Capacity Management also allow businesses to eliminate redundant work and ensure consistent reporting, tweak IT applications and infrastructure components to improve performance and reduce consumption, and more importantly, get more out of existing IT resources. In addition, a more systematic service level and associated financial information are available to the business through the use of Capacity Management processes. Because of this, Capacity Management teams have close ties to ITIL Service Level Management and Financial Management departments.

Simulating Your ITIL

In production, anything goes, and it is best that businesses anticipate problems before they arise. An ITIL overview simulator is software that allows businesses to predict what is to happen during actual performance. It is software that will show what will transpire if an IT application reaches an abnormal situation, without actually creating the situation. An ITIL overview simulator is designed to monitor the application of the system as it runs and determines what resources it uses. After the observation phase, the list of activities, and creation of environmental faults, are made to simulate failures of these activities. Some ITIL overview simulator software covers the five types of environmental fault: COM, Disk I/O, Memory, Network, and Registry.

The ITIL overview simulator allows businesses to check on their performance and improve them for better results. Some of the benefits that an ITIL overview simulator software provides to IT service management are as follows:

- To be able to predict the course and results of certain actions.
- To have an understanding of why events occur.
- To be able to identify problem areas before implementation.
- To explore results of the modifications made.
- To be able to confirm the known variables.
- To be able to evaluate ideas and identify the reasons behind inefficiencies.
- To gain insight and stimulate one's creative thinking.
- To be able to communicate the simulation results with integrity and feasibility of your proposals.

Make a stepwise refinement in your ITIL implementation, start to simulate events and find solutions even before the problems occur.

CSIP: ITIL Planning To Implement Service Management

ITIL planning to implement service management falls under the service management process of ITIL. It is primarily concerned with providing businesses guidelines on how to align the current business IT infrastructure with future business IT needs and requirements. The ITIL planning to implement service management will develop guidelines for the Continuous Service Improvement Program (CSIP), which will include creating a vision, analysis of the organization, setting of goals, implementation of IT service management and measuring and evaluating progress through the use of Key Performance Indicators (KPI).

If organizations are embarking on an ITIL planning to implement service management, it should be understood that they have fully adopted the ITIL framework of best practice approaches, and have a clear understanding of the service management concepts.

Basic questions need to be answered in planning to implement service management in ITIL. The first and most important would be answering what the vision is. A vision statement will create a purpose for the CSIP, and will bring about commitment from the individuals and empower everyone involved in the project.

After creating a vision, the next step in ITIL planning to implement service management is to determine the current IT infrastructure; analyze where it is now, and where it wants to be in the future. This will determine the service management and stakeholders' maturity. By carefully mapping out and analyzing the current IT organization, the company can then set goals in achieving its future requirements, and fully define where they want to be with regards to future roles based on current assessment.

Once the management has created a vision, analyzed it and set goals, it is then time to implement the IT service management. It should be clear, empowering, well communicated and with a clear sense of accountability. This way, your ITIL planning to implement service management can have measurable goals that can be evaluated.

The ITIL planning to service management is just one of the many ITIL processes. All businesses should have a program for continuous improvement so future requirements are expected.

Learning ITIL through Poster usage

Going over the core volumes of the ITIL v3 may be tedious for those who are not so much into reading, and it is also a rather heavy tome. Others prefer handy materials when studying and make things simple if summarized.

ITIL poster has been developed to aid in understanding the IT service management without necessarily having to stick one's head into reading volumes of books. ITIL poster presents a clear overview of the ITIL structure and its processes. It provides the individual process areas, structure, maturity levels and capability levels of ITIL. It provides a graphical map showing the practical linkage Service Delivery and Service Support processes.

The normal size of an ITIL poster is A3, and is a double-sided laminated map. ITIL poster is not only an aid for those learning or understanding ITIL, but it also allows others in the organization to become aware of the types of management in the IT service. It provides readers the chance to see how IT service management works in an organization and serves as a point of reference too, for those who fail to trace back or recall some of the ITIL concepts.

ITIL poster can be customized based on the organization's objective. An ITIL Process map may be used to show the IT service management flow. This process map serves as an awareness campaign to employees as well as to customers. ITIL poster most of all reminds the organization of the framework that it should apply in keeping the IT service excellent.

ITIL PPT File: The Best Way to Create ITIL Presentations

The Microsoft PowerPoint software application is a popular choice for presentations, as it has graphical slides of different templates that one can choose from. The slides themselves can be printed out, or displayed on-screen with the use of a projector. Microsoft PowerPoint provides three types of movements: (1) entrance; (2) emphasis; and (3) exit. The file can then be saved in a ppt format. The latest version of the software is Microsoft Power-Point 2007.

There are a lot of companies that use Microsoft PowerPoint when creating tutorials to introduce a product, or to better understand the components and functions of a certain process, such as the sets of best practices that represent the Information Technology Infrastructure Library (ITIL). ITIL presentations are made to give the viewer a detailed perspective about the terms and conditions of ITIL, as well as its contribution to the success of an IT-based company. ITIL presentations are also transferred from one company to another as a means of communication. It can also act as a persuasive approach in letting other companies know about the benefits of ITIL.

With the use of colorful texts, pictures, charts, tables and other graphics, an ITIL presentation will indeed amaze the audience, and it will surely make it easier for them to understand ITIL. There are currently some web sites that offer downloadable ppt files about ITIL for free, while some offer it at a reasonable cost, depending on the quality of the presentation. This also serves as a foundation from which one can start learning ITIL and pursue certification courses in the future.

ITIL Procedures: The De Facto Standards for IT Operations

ITIL procedures are the best practices specified on the Information Technology Infrastructure Library that were established for the purpose of making conscious efforts to secure financial value and quality in information technology (IT) operations. These defined steps will help organizations achieve desired results by being guided by the principles behind the development, infrastructure and operational implementation of different IT processes. It is indeed advantageous if all ITIL procedures are being followed. However, employees handling such processes should also have an in-depth knowledge and understanding about the ins and outs of ITIL, so therefore proper training is needed to ensure project success.

In September of 2007, ITIL V3 was published. The latest version of ITIL is comprised of six (6) key volumes, namely:
- Introduction to the ITIL Service Life Cycle;
- Service Strategy;
- Service Design;
- Service Transition;
- Service Operation; and
- Continual Service Improvement.

At present, people who would like to get an ITIL certification should pass the ITIL V3 exam. These six (6) modules were taken from ITIL V2 iteration, while still making it more comprehensive in the realm of IT Service Management (ITSM).

ITIL was able to standardize the vocabulary of information technology infrastructure and processes. Because of this, many organizations have adopted it, and that is the one true reason why

ITIL procedures are so recognized and widely-accepted throughout the world. Successful ITIL implementation needs the involvement of every team member. Everyone should get onboard and pull in the same direction. At the end of the day, it is all about a matter of choice. If the right people lead the right way, while everyone else gives their fair share, then everything will fall into place.

ITIL Demo Process: The Jigsaw Diagram

Companies adopting ITIL best practices are on the rise because it is a proven cost- effective, efficient way for IT managers to maximize control of their IT infrastructure. The ITIL process follows two diagrams: ITIL Jigsaw and the ITIL BS15000. The ITIL process demo diagram explained below is the Jigsaw Diagram, and is one of the two diagrams used by ITIL training schools today.

The Jigsaw Diagram shows five principal elements of ITIL drawn like a jigsaw puzzle. The concept of this ITIL process demo diagram is that the major elements of ITIL can be linked together like a jigsaw puzzle -- some of the pieces may fit perfectly and some may not. The overlapping pieces represent the need to integrate each process of the diagram. They are the business perspective, service delivery, service support, ICT infrastructure management and applications management.

The business perspective illustrates the strategic level of the ITIL Jigsaw, and will discuss the issues of continuity management, partnerships, change survival and change in business practices.

Service delivery covers the management of the applications in a tactical level, and will include capacity management, financial management for IT services, service level management, availability management and continuity of IT service. If continuous service delivery is important, service support will equally be just as important because it ensures that the customer or user has continuous access to the IT service. Service support covers the service desk, incident, problem, configuration, release and change management.

ICT infrastructure management is the core of service delivery and support while the applications management identifies the issues of change and will provide a solution to the situation.

The Jigsaw Diagram is an ITIL process demo diagram that shows how different pieces fit together to form one common goal.

Understanding Basic Concepts through ITIL Process Demo

Employees within an organization are most likely unaware that there is such a term as Information Technology Infrastructure Library (ITIL). It is also possible that it is currently being implemented within the organization, but most people still do not have a sound knowledge about ITIL. There are even companies that see the importance of an ITIL certification as a requirement for entry level employment or promotion, depending on what position is available. Though it is indeed a bit complex to understand the different processes revolving around ITIL, there are also a lot of books available for everyone to read. However, it is still advisable to enroll in an actual ITIL training course. Aside from the fact that only enrollees of ITIL training courses are eligible to take an ITIL certification exam, being in a classroom setting is still better because it is more interactive; you can participate in discussions with the facilitator and co-students, and it will eventually generate an in-depth understanding of ITIL.

As beginners, there are also ITIL process demos available on the internet. ITIL process demos are good sources of information, giving you a glimpse of the basics of ITIL, its functions and processes. You can consider this as a baseline in learning new things until you become an expert on ITIL. Viewing these demos will also make it easier for you to understand the entire process when you are already trying for your ITIL certification. With determination, coupled with positive thinking and a good working knowledge of ITIL, getting IT certification will be more than achievable.

ITIL Process Diagram: Jigsaw and BS15000

As previously mentioned, the ITIL process diagrams have two illustrations: the Jigsaw Diagram and the BS15000. The Jigsaw ITIL process diagram shows us five principal elements, which are represented by an illustration of a jigsaw puzzle with the pieces overlapping each other. These overlapping elements establish the importance of integrating all the elements in order to achieve one common goal. The five principal elements are the business perspective, applications management, IT services delivery, IT services support and infrastructure management. The jigsaw diagram was formulated with the assistance of service management groups and organizations.

BS15000 ITIL process diagram was conceptualized by the British Standards Institute and basically has the same elements as the jigsaw diagram except for the details and explanation. Both have ITIL principles for service management.

Service management is the core of both the Jigsaw and BS15000 ITIL process diagrams. Both are primarily concerned with delivering the services and support that are needed by the IT business. Surrounding service management are other ITIL disciplines that include the implementation of service management, business perspective, management of ICT infrastructure and application management.

The ITIL process diagram categorizes service management into different processes that can be a function or a discipline in itself (like change management, configuration management, incident management, etc.). Different processes they may be, but they all show the importance of how they are all interrelated, overlapping and are integrated with each other.

Whatever ITIL process diagram an IT organization may choose, both the Jigsaw and the BS15000 need to be custom filled with the needs of the company, and may appear different from the original. But when viewed as a whole, they will still be a complete ITIL solution.

ITIL Flow Process on Live Demo

Business organizations should look into improving the quality of service to customers as well as to their employees. A growing company should ensure that the quality of the product or service provided is improved, cost reduction is considered, proactively manage the IT infrastructure information, and well-define its IT processes. A vital aspect of an IT service management involves the proper managing of its IT resources in an automated and centralized way.

The Configuration Management Databases (CMDB), which is the central repository of the management process of an organization, is focused on the management of incident, change and problem management. Monitoring these has become difficult when done manually and so software has been made available to make it easier for organizations. An ITIL process flow live demo allows ITIL users to clearly understand the ITIL concepts and processes, as well as provide aids in handling problems within the management process. An example is the CMDB, wherein the software is used to register all IT assets including hardware, software, contracts, service level agreements, relevant information, and complete management of each component's unique lifecycle. It also includes an audit log and history of change of the IT assets. The tapping or access to the configuration management database (CMDB) and IT assets are secured, and access is given only to authorized personnel. The ITIL process flow live demo is software that, if bought, allows management to change constituents for approval, and allows configurable reports to be accessible for top management to read.

Tools to Aid ITIL Process

While the ITIL has been internationally accepted as the standard guidelines in the IT service management, not much has been told on how to handle the processes. The ITIL processes are the best practices to manage any problems with the processes.

Three of the ITIL tools used are:

- Process management tools: refers to the management processes of ITIL and tracking of its statuses, assignments, escalations, historical work performed, and tasks relative to fulfilling the work.
- Analysis Tools: refers to tools needed in analyzing relevant data. It enables a detailed understanding of metrics that aim to assist in providing accurate completion tasks.
- Execution Tools: refers to tools use to enable personnel responsible to complete the task using automated solutions.

The above tools are used in the implementation of the four processes of ITIL, as well as in fine-tuning and adjusting controls to meet an organization's needs. The tools actually list down the actual tasks that should be performed to support each activity. For example, an ITIL Change Management would have great effect on the personnel or group personnel concerned. The request for the change should be validated and would require checking as to whether such a change is justifiable. The ITIL process tools are used toward coming up with a final decision whether change should be made or not.

With the ITIL process tools on hand, documenting and finding immediate solutions to IT problems will be easier to handle. It is through the ITIL process tools that an organization can minimize a cost to its IT budget, or how much revenue it can earn from giving quick responses to its users.

Service Support and Service Delivery - The Two Significant Disciplines Involved in the ITIL Process

ITIL involves a lot of processes that have specific functions within the organization. Each has its own role in ensuring that the ITIL standards are in place; so as to generate more desired results, not only for customers but also for the company as well. ITIL process improvement is also something that the company should consider, especially on the Service Support ITIL discipline. Since Service Support is the one that is close to the users and/or customers, constant feedback is often generated. This is especially true when users want changes to the system, want to incorporate new features and update them once they're available, wants to ask for inquiries, and needs help when difficulties arise.

Another process, called Service Delivery, should also be taken into consideration. In it, the company should make sure that all services specified on the agreement (SLA) are given to the customer. Failure to do so will result in disputes and misunderstandings that can only lead to unfavorable circumstances between the two parties.

The Service Delivery and Service Support disciplines are the components of the ITIL Service Management (ITSM). There are a lot of ITIL training courses that are dedicated to emphasizing the importance of ITSM in promoting the various practices that lean toward customer satisfaction. Though constant feedback from the customer is necessary in developing ITIL process improvements, it is still a must to promote a good working relationship with them, and encourage communication in order to eliminate false expectations. When the agreement has been established, the company should still think of the best possible starting point for the IT service improvement efforts. Customer satisfaction, coupled with improved service will definitely come a long way.

ITIL Quiz/Exam: The Biggest Challenge for Potential ITIL Professionals

To be a distinguished professional in the field of Information Technology Infrastructure Library (ITIL), you must take training courses to have a working knowledge of the basic concepts of ITIL, as well as an in-depth understanding about its processes and functions. However, you need to achieve first an ITIL certification by taking ITIL quizzes or exams at recognized centers. This is one of the biggest challenges that you have, aside from deciding on what career level you will aspire to in the future.

The ITIL quiz/exam usually comes in a simplified multiple choice format, wherein you select the best possible answer for the question presented. The level of toughness depends on the certification level that you are applying for. More often than not, you will receive the results and certificate within four weeks after the examination session. There is no limit to the number of times you can retake the ITIL quiz/exam, if you failed to get a passing score.

Many people consider taking up ITIL training courses mainly for career and personal development reasons. If you're considering a change of career path, ITIL certification is needed, since most advertised job postings require it as a prerequisite, if not an extra qualification that will put your resume on top of the pile. To acquire basic knowledge about ITIL, there are a lot of training manuals available for you to read. However, it is still the best option to attend an accredited training course for intermediate or diploma levels.

ITIL Salary Increases with Certification

An individual who can present an ITIL certificate demonstrates his seriousness in dealing with and resolving service management issues. ITIL is the most adopted service management best practice today. Although the ITIL salary will vary upon the different areas of expertise, any experience in the field of ITIL application will definitely be an advantage to anyone.

If you are applying as ITIL project manager, you should know and understand the needs of the clients and the business as well. Developing IT processes and strategies, handling projects and managing the approval of processes in IT are just some of the major responsibilities of a project manager in ITIL.

Certification plays a great part in Information Technology, especially in ITIL. This could affect your capability and your value in the ITIL job market. ITIL provides different certifications for each type of training. The most basic would be the ITIL Foundation Certificate, followed by the ITIL Practitioner Certificate, and then the ITIL Manager Certificate. Additional certificates of the latest ITIL v3 are now also being offered, which could further increase your value to the IT marketplace.

Some companies provide a very competitive tax-free salary, paid holidays, healthcare provision, accommodations and perks such as free laptop and cell phone. Companies can provide big bonuses if you qualify for their needs. The salary for an ITIL Project Manager is roughly around $80,000 and $90,000 in the US. This is the going rate for ITIL managers who have a proven track record in handling, monitoring, and implementing IT service management projects.

ITIL Security Management: Increasing the Company's Level of Security

Security can either make or break a company's reputation. If taken seriously, rest assured, the customers will feel at ease in providing confidential data, which means continued business. This also applies to company rules and policies, as only authorized users are granted access to such top secret information. But then, if security is taken for granted, it also means a threat to the company. Leaving relevant information unsafe to possible fictitious and fraudulent sources will result to a lot of law suits due to security glitches, leaving the company at its lowest point. This is why a lot of preventive measures were adapted to increase the level of security within the organization. In information technology, ITIL Security Management is the answer.

ITIL Security Management is intended to make sure that the security aspects of services are provided at a level that is agreeable to both the service provider and the customer. It provides a common and well-understood concept to both parties, in such a way that they will have a better understanding of the reasons behind the needed security policies and procedures.

Based on the Code of Practice for information security management (ISO/IEC 17799), ITIL Security Management is divided into two parts. First is the realization of the security requirements, as written in the Service Level Agreement (SLA), and other external requirements that are specified in other contracts or policies. Second is the realization of a basic level of security to guarantee the continuity of the organization and reach a simplified level of Service Level Management for information security.

Service Delivery: Capacity Management in ITIL

Capacity management ensures that the business is able to deliver existing and future IT infrastructure requirements at the right moment, right time and in the most cost-effective way. Capacity management falls under the Service Delivery of ITIL and involves three other sub-processes: Business Capacity Management, Service Capacity Management and Resource Capacity Management. In ITIL v3, Resource Capacity Management was renamed Component Capacity Management.

IT is ever expanding and growing, and requirements in terms of processing power, memory and other hardware components immediately follow. Without capacity management, businesses will continually make unnecessary upgrades resulting in unwanted expenses. But with capacity management or ITIL, these will be eliminated because organizations will be able to monitor, analyze and fine-tune current server load, and then properly predict how and what the demands will be over time.

Organizations which choose to implement capacity management or ITIL in their businesses will reap the long-term benefits of their investment. By being proactive in their approach to business needs, rather than reactive, organizations can maximize their IT resources and increase performance of applications and infrastructure components by proper performance analysis of existing and new releases.

Organizations will also be able to get rid of redundant work by fine-tuning the performance of existing infrastructure, and identifying the most efficient way to use it. With an efficient infrastructure, organizations will be more accurate and consistent in their reporting, which will enable them to make informed business decisions and plans.

Being less reactive, capacity management or ITIL will save the company unnecessary expenses because it identifies the possible sources of business growth hindrances and can immediately provide corrective actions before it happens.

ITIL Service Support and Processes

ITIL Service Support is just one of the two disciplines of IT Service Management. It includes the support procedures to make sure that service quality is implemented. These procedures handle the problems and changes in the IT framework. There are six main processes that are included in this framework. They are the following:

- Help Desk: is a tracking procedure that helps with client requests and problems. This area is responsible for distributing information to your company about any intended changes that can make an impact to operations and other production procedures.
- Incident Management: focuses on the re-establishment of services following an incident. This process is first and foremost a □reactive□ process. This procedure provides the supervision on analytical procedures that is necessary to restore the company's services. The Incident Management processes are incorporated with Help Desk/Service Desk.
- The Problem Management: concentrates on recognizing the causes of service issues. This identifies the commission corrective work to prevent repetition of incidents. Problem Management plays a vital role in getting and examining data.
- Configuration Management: processes the report and archiving of individual infrastructure. This process works closely with the Change Management process. Risk assessments must take into account the relationships that may have an effect on operations and production processes.

- Change Management: manages any change that is presented into the IT framework. It evaluates the risks in changes, recognizes the dependencies and other changes that create impacts on systems and applications. It is said to be successful if the changes are incorporated into production operation without any negative effects on your business.
- Release Management: attends to large scale changes in the IT environment. This includes installing the latest database management system and managing extensive changes to your company's application. It manages big amounts of changes that will be brought into the production operating environment.

These processes in ITIL Service Support are very important in creating dynamic IT system and applications. They will help your company in serving satisfied customers.

ITIL Training: Defining the Different ITIL Certification Courses

To gain knowledge and expertise on a certain subject, extensive training is needed wherein everything related to the chosen topic is discussed in detail. At first, we see training as classroom discussions facilitated by a speaker or trainer. But now, since everything is almost high-tech, training courses can now be taken online at your most convenient time. The same is true with Information Technology Infrastructure Library (ITIL) training, as there are a lot of web sites that offer such services. The three levels of ITIL training that are normally accredited are: Foundations Certificate Course, Practitioners Certificate Course and Managers Certificate Course.

A Foundations Certificate Course is like a basic training course, wherein students are given an overview on ITIL, its objectives and benefits; as well as the definition of terms and concepts needed to clearly understand the processes and functions involved in the ITIL best practice framework.

A Practitioners Certificate Course is like a second-level course, and focuses on discussions needed to gain a more in-depth understanding about the different activities involved in ITIL. This is more of a training guide to people who will soon work on, or are currently working within, a specific ITIL process.

On the other hand, the Managers Certificate Course is the highest level of ITIL training, wherein the individual, who should be at a Managerial position, has at least five years of working knowledge in IT. This course focuses on developing the vision of making use of ITIL within the organization. It also covers discussions about dealing with changes within the organization, and how to overcome and manage such changes to your advantage.

ITIL V3: From Process to Service Life Cycle

An organization working with a computerized environment should have regular updates to the management of their IT resources. The IT Infrastructure Library (ITIL) is the standard framework of the best IT practices. As technology grows, there is a need for more development. ITIL version 2 gave focus to the process cycle. This then gave rise to ITIL v3. It placed focus on the service life cycle, establishing importance to business value rather than in the execution processes.

ITIL v3 core volumes are:

- Service Strategy deals with identification as to the type of services to be marketed based on the needs of internal or external customers. This volume covers areas in Service Portfolio Management and Financial Management.
- Service Design deals with how the strategy should take place through creation of a design document to cover aspects that require support. This volume covers areas in Availability Management, Capacity Management, Continuity Management and Security Management.
- Service Transition deals with the implementation of the strategy, and the creation of a product service or modification of an existing service. This volume covers area in Change Management, Release Management, Configuration Management and Service Knowledge Management.
- Service Operation deals with activities necessary in the service and maintenance of operations. Ensuring

that requirements as defined in the Service Level Agreements are met. This volume covers areas in Incident Management, Problem Management and Request Fulfillment.

- Continual Service Improvement deals with continuous delivery of quality service to customers. This volume covers the areas in Service Reporting, Service Measurement and Service Level Management.

Delivery of product or services is not enough, quality of service is most important factor in moving your company toward business success.

ITIL and White Papers in PPT

Knowledge is based on what you have learned either through reading or experience. Most often we gather information through reading books, articles from newspapers and magazines, and from online information such as wikipedia etc. With online information, how can one be assured that such information are factual and provide authoritative reports? Nowadays a new form of information provided through website readers is white paper ppt.

In an IT service management, ITIL white paper is now the commonly used authoritative report for providing information on the framework structure of the ITIL and the best practices in the IT services. ITIL is used to educate customers as well as companies in making decisions about improving their IT service management.

ITIL white paper ppt should be carefully crafted so as not to mislead others that it was written for marketing purposes. The ITIL white paper should be accomplished by giving an educational content that would be relevant to interested readers. It should focus on the reader's need in getting specific solutions from the sponsor paper. The ITIL white paper ppt should provide an extensive discussion on what has been gained from advanced IT service management solutions and how ITIL is to be implemented. The paper should provide the procedural steps to planning, selecting and implementing ITIL out of the box and into the management level.

The ITIL white paper is sponsored by white paper vendors. It is normally accessed through power point or the Adobe player version.

Customize Your ITIL Workflow

It pays to have a system working on the things you do in life. Just in carrying out activities, you follow steps until you meet your objectives. In businesses, especially in the production of goods or services you follow a pattern. This repeated pattern of activities is called workflow. ITIL being the standard guideline observed by both the public and private sector in their IT departments, service providers have also come up with an ITIL workflow to have a better understanding of the IT processes in IT service management. The ITIL workflow is a repeated pattern of activities that allows an organization to have a systematic way of using their resources, and defining the roles, mass, energy and information flows that result from a work process that is documented and learned.

ITIL workflow software has been made available for organizations to create their own work processes following the standard guidelines of ITIL. End users of the ITIL workflow can create a workflow even without programming skills. The ITIL workflow software completely automates the activities, from the time the system has forwarded (via email) the tasks and approvals to the assigned officers or group recipients. The system automatically processes the task and approvals, and progresses to the next task or approval, and so on 'til finality.

The use of the ITIL workflow software allows users a better understanding of the IT work process, and how things should be handled within the IT departments. The ITIL workflow software can be an effective tool as you improve the reliability and the organization's responsiveness on providing IT services and processes. It can also give your organization a fast turnaround on change and reduce the rework or duplicated efforts of your organization, thus reducing implementation costs as well.

A Short Definition of ITIL Best Practice

If we rely on the regular meaning of the words Best Practice, it may lead us to thinking that Best Practice refers to a job performance rating. However, ITIL Best Practice actually pertains to areas intended for application of the service management concepts. These areas are listed in a series of informative books which provide guidance on how IT services should be implemented properly. Below is a list of Best Practice functions and a brief description of each.

Service Support relates to five areas of discipline such as Configuration Management; Problem Management; Change Management; Help Desk; and Software Control and Distribution. These areas enable IT Services to be provided.

Service Delivery is the management of IT services itself. Under Service Delivery would be: Service Level Management; Capacity Management; Contingency Management; Availability Management; and Cost Management for IT Services. These areas allow us a snapshot of the role of Service Delivery management, which is to ensure that the overall efficiency of delivery of services to customers can be sustained.

The area of Planning to Implement Service Management is an important ITIL framework. Its job is to align the business needs with IT resources. It therefore includes the following necessary elements in analysis: create a vision; help in analysis of the organization; support setting goals, facilitate implementation of IT services; and allow measurement of goals.

ICT Infrastructure Support and Management provides the necessary support in line with Best Practice guidance on any requirements needed. These include: planning, design, testing, deployment, operations necessitating technical support, and management.

ITIL Application Management identifies the service level requirements of the business. Through it, ITIL can then be used to standardize the business procedures in accordance with ITIL Best Practice.

Lastly, The Business Perspective involves looking at how IT resources can be incorporated into the business from the perspective of how the business normally operates. It should effectively merge the preferred technology with the needs of the people being served if the business needs are truly understood.

The Scope of ITIL Best Practices

The Information Technology Infrastructure Library (ITIL) was developed to provide assistance and guidance to IT professionals and their respective employers as far as the scope of IT infrastructure, development and operations are concerned.

It is a framework of best practices designed to facilitate the delivery of Information Technology (IT) services by companies who work in the IT field. Its high-quality and extensive management procedures help clients (such as businesses) and end users get the best value they can from their internal and external IT operations.

ITIL best practices are concerned with the services rendered by IT service providers in the areas of Service Support; Service Delivery; Planning to Implement Service Management; ICT Infrastructure Management; Application Management and The Business Perspective. The two most frequently utilized services are the Service Support and the Service Delivery.

Service Support enables the IT Services to be effectively utilized. It covers five basic areas. The first is Configuration Management, which offers the implementation database that contains the necessary information needed by the business to effectively use IT services in the areas of maintenance, movement and problems with configuration items. The basic function of Problem Management (the second area) is to provide resolution and prevention of problems that may cause delays in the smooth flow of operation of an organization using IT services. The third area is Change Management, which was designed to assist the first area (Configuration Management). Here, changes to the IT system should be planned and authorized before being implemented. Next is Help Desk Management, which is known as the most frequently used service.

This is where front liners serve customers via the help desk. The fifth is the area of Software Control and Distribution, which is simply management of software development, installation and support.

Service Delivery covers the management of IT services. These include: Service Level Management; Capacity Management; Contingency Planning, Availability Management and Cost Management for IT Services. All of these areas of discipline in IT were designed to provide best service in the area of total management of IT services to guarantee smooth operations for client companies and end users.

Change Advisory Board of ITIL

The Change Advisory Board (or CAB) is a group that assesses any request for changes regarding the needs of the business, its priorities, the benefits and cost, and the possible impact of the change to the other systems and operations. Usually, the recommendations for any implementation, further evaluation and analysis, postponement and cancellation are done by the CAB. It is comprised of groups of people who offer expert advice to the Change Management team about the implementation of the changes. The board is made up of representatives from all of the divisions in Information Technology, and other representatives coming from the business units, and any parties outside the premises of the organization that are considered necessary.

The change process in ITIL gives the full responsibility to the CAB regarding the assessment and evaluation of the processes that are submitted, and are subjected for approval and immediate implementation. The function of the CAB takes place during plenary meetings, and not in the planning process and implementation. Its role is limited to only the approval, update and assessment of the process.

Frequent meetings call for approval of the change, and it does not mean that change is altered by the failure of the scope of the proposal. In cases where change is accompanied by failure, another meeting is held and another approval is required. The Change Advisory Board is very close to the planning and implementation process. Its common approach is to assess and approve the implementation of alternative procedures and use the ones that will surely work and are free of failure.

The ITIL Capacity Process

The Capacity Management of ITIL is only one of the five components of the Service Delivery area of ITIL. The nature of the work is not reactive, but proactive. It is responsible for ensuring that the needs of the business and the definition of the services are fulfilled using the minimum measurement of resources. The process of Capacity Management involves monitoring, tuning, analyzing and implementing the changes necessary in the utilization of the resources. It also involves managing the demand for the measurement of resources that requires the understanding of the priorities of the business. Modeling is a process of Capacity Management used for the simulation of the performance of the infrastructure and to know the future needs of the resources.

The measurement of applications should be understood to make sure that the service levels required are met by the company. This is also a process involved in the ITIL management of capacity for any organization.

The company is required to produce a capacity plan documented with all the current utilization and future requirements, as well as the cost of the new releases and new applications. There is also a need for the organization, as a part of their capacity process, to make an annual growth plan for its infrastructure with all the inputs coming from other teams within the organization.

The need for the implementation of Capacity Management in an organization is very important, since ITIL capacity management gives a fast and early win that generated cost savings that can eventually be used for future ITIL projects of the company. The benefits of Capacity Management make it a good candidate for the first implementation in the Service Delivery area of ITIL.

The Benefits of Using an ITIL Case Study

The continuous desire of the people behind ITIL to improve ITIL-related technology so that end users will benefit has led to the compilation of individual case studies (based on frequently-encountered problems). Basically, ITIL case studies zero in on the problem areas encountered by ITIL practitioners. The basic framework of ITIL itself, the series of books and information now available about IT management, coupled with the actual data of each case cited allows readers to gain a clearer idea of the scope and more in-depth analysis of the case.

When a customer contacts the help desk, most likely he has encountered a problem serious enough to bring to the attention of the help desk experts. Every case presented to the help desk team must be treated promptly and with precision. Since record keeping is done electronically, every case can later be reviewed for future reference. ITIL provides the maximum support in the integration of people, processes and the Information Technology into one seamless system. Reading the ITIL case studies provides an opportunity for IT staff to improve on their application of technology. These cases can show whether the problem was due to implementation, or is inherent to the technology itself. Either way, improvement of the system should be pursued.

What are the benefits that a company can derive from distributing an ITIL case study to its IT staff? First and foremost, customer satisfaction will probably increase. One dissatisfied customer will probably result to a hundred more (if the underlying problem is not addressed directly). The team must learn to be proactive in cases caused by technical glitches. Take care of the problem before the customers even detect it. Eventually, the organization may find that IT infrastructure complaints or failures will be reduced by such a policy. Cost reduction is another benefit the company can get from learning from case studies. Since developing procedures and practices within the organization costs money, if the IT personnel learn from the case studies, that is a good investment.

When information is organized and prepared into ITIL case studies, the staff gains the confidence to face customers because they know they are well prepared. This may result in better communication between the customers and the IT staff. Most of all, standards can be improved with the ultimate goal of guaranteeing customer satisfaction.

How to Pass an ITIL Case Study Exam

The ITIL Manager's Certificate represents a step forward for IT personnel to the prized ITIL managerial career. If you are pursuing the ITIL Manager's Certificate, this means that you have already completed the ITIL Foundation Certificate, and are now prepared to face the much more challenging career of an ITIL Service Manager. You should understand, though, that you will be facing an exam that will test your ability to analyze IT-related problems as well as your capability for managing ITIL-based solutions used in Service Management.

Normally, the exam consists of one general question and four process questions. There is no doubt that you could easily answer the general question, but since an ITIL Service Manager is responsible for a number of areas of disciplines in ITIL, you should prepare by reading ITIL case studies, since you do not know which area will be covered specifically. You have to be prepared if ITIL case studies are also included in the exam.

Reviewing adequately is the key. You have to be familiar with different cases covering the different areas of concern that an ITIL Manager may encounter, such as Service and Delivery. Make use of the available reviewers from your training provider. Try to simulate a real-life exam situation. Practice answering case problems under time pressure. Getting used to the exam scenario will make the actual exams less stressful.

Read and understand thoroughly any ITIL case study you may come across. Get into the heart of the case and do not linger on the sidelights too long. Your resources should be devoted to covering as many problems as you possibly can, without sacrificing quality. Be focused on the case study you choose, without being distracted by minor data that are merely incidental to the real issue. Always base your solutions on the ITIL Best Practice discipline. You will also be able to maximize your chances of passing if you are able to see the exam through the eyes of the examiner or exam creator.

What Should I do to Earn an ITIL Certificate?

We know that the Information Technology Infrastructure Library (ITIL) is a set of best practices for IT. It is a registered trademark of the United Kingdom Office of Government Commerce (OGC). ITIL was created by the UK government Central Computer and Telecommunications Agency (CCTA) back in the 1980s and is now known as the OGC. Its creation was meant to support the efficient use of IT services and resources, and it was later updated to what we know as the different ITIL versions.

The phenomenal worldwide growth and acceptance of ITIL was indeed remarkable, and gave businesses around the world the technology they need. ITIL is now globally used and fully supported by different independent agencies with training courses including exams and certifications. IT professionals have to undergo additional education and training in certain ITIL areas of concern to be able to take the examination, and thus be awarded with a certification given by either EXIN or ISEB. Both of these providers are globally-recognized and independent ITIL examination providers.

The IT professional who has undergone training for the first time can be happy to know that the ITIL Foundation Certificate awaits him at the end. This certificate is a prerequisite for the ITIL Practitioner Certificate and/or the ITIL Manager's Certificate. Being an ITIL Foundation Certificate recipient means the IT professional understands the terminology used within ITIL, and is knowledgeable of the basic ITIL Service Support and Service Delivery systems, as well as the generic ITIL philosophy.

An ITIL Practitioner Certificate holder is fully competent in the applications of different processes within the IT Service Management discipline.

And the ITIL Manager's Certificate is given to those who pass the appropriate exam, and have professional experience in the field of management. This person will be entrusted in managing service management areas after certification.

The Importance of ITIL Certifications

The ITIL is a series of documents created by the UK government to promote and implement an efficient framework for IT service management (also called ITSM). This framework defines and organizes a system of network management within individual user organizations. It is devoted to establishing consistency in standards that help businesses improve on their core competencies by letting certified ITIL personnel handle their IT infrastructure in-house.

There are three levels under ITIL certification. First is the Foundation Certificate, second is the Practitioner Certificate, and third is the Manager's Certificate.

The Foundation Certificate is awarded to a person who understands the terms used within the world of ITIL. It focuses on the basic knowledge applied to Information Technology Infrastructure Library services, support and service delivery; as well as the general ITIL philosophy and background. It is a mandatory certificate that you need to attain before you may aspire to both the Practitioner and the Manager's certificates in IT Service Management.

The Practitioner Certificate focuses on your understanding of the function of a specific process within the IT service management discipline. Having a Practitioner Certificate implies that you are a specialist in design and implementation of ITIL procedures.

The last certificate, called The Manager's Certificate, goes to the most experienced professionals who are involved in managerial service functions. They are responsible for the set-up and execution of ITIL from the top down.

Relying on ITIL will help organizations keep their costs to a minimum; assure quick results; segregate staff concerned with technical issues from those who are of a non-technical capacity; and give them the ability to measure technical support performance.

Do My IT People Need to Be ITIL Certified?

The ITIL (Information Technology Infrastructure Library) is now being accepted globally, catering to different organizations based on their IT needs. It is composed of a series of documents, originally created and owned by the Office of the Government of Commerce of the United Kingdom. It was created to support the implementation of an efficient framework for IT Service Management. IT professionals are nowadays required to be equipped with the global standard in knowledge of IT technology, which usually means being ITIL certified.

The growing need to be updated about developments in IT technology has encouraged career IT professionals to get more in-depth knowledge about the world of IT. However, standardization of the technology was needed so that professionals desiring to enter the field would be adequately informed, tested and then certified. A 40-question multiple-choice exam must be taken by these IT people before any of them can be issued an ITIL Foundation Certificate. A holder of this Certificate is certified to be equipped with the foundational knowledge in ITIL Service Support, Service Delivery and the various terminologies of ITIL. With a Foundation Certificate safe in hand, the ITIL career ladder may then lead to two other branches of ITIL: the Practitioner Certificate (involved in the application of IT Service Management) and, of course, the Manager's Certificate.

When you are ITIL Certified, that means that you have sufficient skills to support IT-dependent organizations in their quest to present a comprehensive set of management procedures to help them (and their client organizations) in the management of their IT operation. ITIL supports IT service providers in the planning of consistent, documented and frequently used processes. These improve the quality and promptness of service delivery. It is essential for the IT professional who is aspiring for ITIL certification to be fully knowledgeable about his craft as IT is synonymous with swift, standard and accurate quality service.

What Benefits will You Get from Taking an ITIL Course?

Working in a company that deals with the IT industry requires you to be updated with the latest that technology has to offer. Information Technology Infrastructure Library is a set of guidelines, and is a solid framework that you can use in your organization to ensure that high quality services will be provided to your clients. Now, in order for you to learn everything about ITIL, you can study about the principles and take an exam for the ITIL Foundation Certification, or take tests in ITIL Version 2 or Version 3, for those who already have basic knowledge of ITIL. Just like when you are studying for any type of professional exam, you can take short courses offered for individuals who would like to be ITIL certified.

ITIL courses are ideal for those who would like to learn more about ITIL that is used by global companies. You may be able to learn about the basics of ITIL all by yourself as you do research and by reading books. However, if you wish to pass the ITIL certification exams to determine your level of knowledge, it will be much more beneficial for you, and for the company that you represent, to take an ITIL course. With an ITIL course, you will learn the basics on ITIL service management. Your business management skills will also be developed, and you will have a deeper understanding of the key ITIL process relationships. By signing up for an ITIL course, you will be able to get that ITIL certification and have a better understanding of how ITIL frameworks, processes and guidelines benefit and assist business all over the world.

eTOM and ITIL

eTOM is a classification for the activities done by the service provider in an organization. When eTOM and ITIL are described, they are both frameworks of a business process for the service providers. Their difference is that eTOM has a wider approach than ITIL, while ITIL focuses on the operational part of the lifecycle of the service. ITIL describes the best practices in a textual way, while eTOM uses an engineering approach since it considers engineering services, the management of orders and sales processes of the organization.

Both ITIL and eTOM frameworks deal with the management of the services and how they are delivered to the customer. ITIL and eTOM are not in conflict with each other. They are in fact mutually supportive, complementary and compatible frameworks. Each of them has its own strengths, which can be used to support and complement the other. The methods that describe how ITIL and eTOM can work together have already been developed and are now demonstrated using sequences of worked samples. Through the use of these, it was identified that the scope of both frameworks overlap in a manner that, when they are used together, they can work successfully.

The best practice guidance of ITIL can be used in identifying a policy for Change Management that can be adopted by some organizations by following the descriptive approach of ITIL. With the use of the eTOM framework, the policy made from ITIL can be embedded usually within the Enterprise Management of an organization. The standard can act as a corporate policy in handling a particular area in the business and eventually flow over the business with the supporting processes of eTOM inline with the particular policy.

What to Expect From ITIL Exams

The Office of Government Commerce of the government of the United Kingdom, which created the Information Technology Infrastructure Library (commonly called ITIL), aims to keep end users updated on developments regarding ITIL. ITIL is a compilation of best practices in the burgeoning field of IT that allows end users to maintain the best possible IT system within their organization.

There are two independent companies that conduct examinations. The first ITIL exam host is the Examination Institute for Information Science (or EXIN). The second is the System Examination Board (or ISEB). These companies develop and organize the exams and conduct ITIL certifications.

Though these companies do not offer courses based in ITIL, there are companies that are dedicated to offering courses concerning ITIL training. These companies also conduct ITIL-related services such as management consultancy in ITIL, and helping examinees prepare for examinations hosted by EXIN or ISEB.

These examinations are necessary to assure test takers adhere to the required ITIL standards while guaranteeing they keep up with service quality standards. By taking either of the tests, you are able to find out how good you are when it comes to ITIL knowledge, and is a stepping stone toward ITIL certification. Through the examinations, you will be conforming to international standards, which in themselves are necessary to avoid confusion in the IT industry among ITIL practitioners.

Companies that prepare ITIL-exam-related courses try to give exams that are as similar as possible to the real thing.

A company that offers these exam-related services focuses on preparing you for certification in ITIL. They offer mock exams that are patterned almost exactly on the same ITIL knowledge base, so that you are assured of optimum performance when it comes to the real exams. These mock exams will uncover your weak points, and they help you to progress so that you can improve over time.

ITIL Foundation Certificate: The Basics

If you are working for a company whose major dealings involve anything and everything about information technology, then it will be beneficial for you to have an ITIL Foundation certificate. Take a look at the following reasons why you need to have an ITIL Foundation certificate to be a bona fide IT professional.

First, it helps to be ITIL qualified because by studying for the certification, you will be more familiar with the best practices used in the IT service management industry and have a background of the ITIL frameworks and guidelines. There are several levels of ITIL certifications, including ITIL Version 2 and ITIL Version 3.

Whether an IT company requires ITIL certification or not, it will still present big career opportunities for you in the future if you pass the ITIL certification exams. For the basic level of ITIL Foundation certification, you will learn about the techniques, methods and processes involved with the deliver of service used by IT companies, as well as information on how they go about their support activities.

With a higher level of ITIL certification, you can use your ITIL foundation principles; apply them to the needs of your own organization, and think of how they can be effectively implemented. With an ITIL Foundation certificate, you can advance your knowledge of the ITIL framework, develop them as you see suitable for your company's needs, and lead the pact in the IT industry.

All About ITIL Foundation Certificate in IT Service Management

Information Technology Infrastructure Library (ITIL) is a framework designed in the 1980's, and over the years, it has been number one in setting the standards for the delivery of top-of-the-line IT services from companies around the globe. If you want to be ITIL certified to advance your knowledge and career in the information technology industry, there are several paths that you can choose from. You can either take the ITIL Foundation Certification exam, the ITIL Version 2, or the ITIL Version 3 exams. Under the ITIL Version 2 category, you can either have an ITIL foundation certificate, an ITIL practitioner's certificate, or an ITIL manager's certificate.

If you decide to advance your knowledge and take on the ITIL Version 2 certification challenge, then you need to learn about two things: service support and service delivery. These are two terms that you will often stumble upon if you want to obtain an ITIL Foundation Certification in IT Service Management. With service support, you will know how management affects a company's service desk and how to efficiently manage or handle your company's IT configuration, and how to proceed when facing a given situation. On the other hand, service delivery will teach you what service delivery is all about, and how to manage your company's IT capacity as well as your finances, service continuity and availability management. All in all, an ITIL Foundation Certification in IT Service Management will give you a clear understanding of how your business, the customers, the management processes, and the industry standards all come together to form a coherent whole.

Sample Questions of ITIL Foundation

The sample questions provided in any ITIL exam help in identifying the strengths and weaknesses of the examinee before taking the actual examination. Sample questions can also aid in improving knowledge regarding the main concepts of the exam. A preparatory kit containing sample questions is made by some well-known ITIL professionals. The kit is usually concise and comprehensive, to assist the examinee in passing the actual ITIL exam. The kit contains a brief introduction about ITIL, some sample questions and their corresponding answers.

Sample questions are basically what the examinee will encounter during the exam itself. They are multiple choice, and require picking the best answer to the specific question. Sample questions are quality guides for the ITIL foundation exam, besides the advice and tips that the examinee can get from the training center, together with all the information they need to support their studies.

Before taking an ITIL foundation exam, the examinee must set in his mind his main purpose in taking the exam. He must also know how to effectively study for the test, and must take into consideration his performance during the sample questioning, so he will have an idea as to how he will perform on the actual exam. He must also think of his next plan after passing the exam, or if he fails.

The success in taking the ITIL exam depends on how the examinee performed during his practice exams, and the way he answered the sample questions of the ITIL foundation.

The ITIL Foundation Exam

The practice tests of ITIL foundation consist of questions that are asked in several ways, but will still arrive at the same answers. The exams can be given by organizations that are reputable when it comes to ITIL exams, and can help you go in the right direction. If you are interested in taking the ITIL exam, what you really need is a good and reliable IT service provider, since they offer different exams for their clients. You can also purchase exams that are provided by accredited organizations. If there are offerings for past ITIL exams, do not believe at once that they are completely accurate; you might put yourself into a not so good situation. There is a big possibility that those exams do not have the correct answers.

After completion of the multiple choice ITIL exam, a certificate will be awarded to you. This certificate can be presented as an entry-level program to take the IT service management certification. You should look for a service provider to give you the exams and the training that is necessary for you to have a good understanding of the practical applications and the framework of ITIL.

Try to consider the following factors when looking for the right IT service provider to give you the ITIL exam: the description of the course, the structure where lectures are provided before taking the exam, and your objective in taking the exam. You must also have the proper knowledge and concept of the ITIL services before you take the exam, so be sure to find the best IT service provider.

Understanding the ITIL Foundations Live Demo

The Information Technology Infrastructure Library (ITIL) is literally a library that contains a series of books which provide vital information about the areas of IT and IT Management. ITIL was developed during the 1980s in the UK; however it was globally adopted in the mid 1990s.

The growing number of users of IT has encouraged many organizations and companies to provide the necessary manpower that can supply technical support functions for the new forms of technology that have come out. An ITIL Foundations live demo is a standard way of presenting the foundational course of ITIL to individuals who may or may not have prior experience and knowledge in ITIL.

ITIL Foundation is an introductory-level course that is intended for IT professionals who would like to prepare themselves for taking the ITIL Foundation Certificate. That certificate is an integral part of the IT Service Management exam. These professionals would be responsible for developing, supporting, and operating application-based IT services and infrastructure-based IT services. An ITIL Foundations live demo must be presented in an informative yet easy to understand way. This must include an overview of ITIL terminologies and structure, as well as basic concepts of the core principles of ITIL for Service Management.

The live presentation must be informative enough so that most (if not all) the basic questions are answered. Every professional who is scouting for the right school or employers should be very discriminating in his choice because it is his career at stake, in the final analysis. It is therefore necessary that the live presentation have content that will convince audiences that the presenter adheres to the global standards of ITIL Foundations.

ITIL Foundations live demos are available on-line, and an on-line staff is available for support. The presenter hosting the high-tech presentation must be knowledgeable and alert enough to provide the necessary information that will satisfy all queries. The point of a live demo is to get prospective IT professionals to sign up for the foundational courses.

Why is the ITIL Incident Management Demo Important?

What is ITIL incident management? It is one part of the ITIL service area of support. It focuses primarily on Incident Management (or IM), which is concerned with restoring services prior to incidents, as promptly as possible. Incident Management basically allows the organization to react by providing guidance in escalating diagnostic procedures required to rapidly restore service.

Incident management includes activities such as: detection and documentation of incident details; classification of the incident and providing initial support; incident matching against previously-encountered problems; resolution of the incident as quickly as possible; prioritization of incidents based on urgency and impact; and escalating the reporting of incidents to other teams to ensure sensible resolution.

The benefits of implementing incident management includes: being able to maintain service levels; meeting demands for service; increasing staff productivity and efficiency; and assuring user satisfaction.

Incidents are classified into three groups: the application area, which includes servicing, application bugs and disk usage; hardware, which is inclusive of system performance, alerts and hardware application; and service requests, which covers information requests, advice and forgotten passwords.

The practice of Incident Management allows the organization to gather real-time support and performance data to provide analysis, which helps to speed up IT tools restoration. Practitioners of incident management monitor activities through data center and incident watching that could highly affect their incident management capabilities. Automatic evaluation of your service application performance, display texts and other indicators are used for detection.

Companies that provide incident management usually offer a demonstration on how they can handle it through the so-called Incident Management Demo. Some of them give at least a 30-day free trial, while others propose an on-line trial instead.

Interactive Live Demo of ITIL

Companies that provide ITIL software, particularly about IT Service Management, can help achieve the ITIL goals of other organizations. Some providers offer consultations regarding ITIL and the training services of ITIL. These providers present interactive live demos of their services and everything that they can do for the organization. Live training sessions and lectures usually consist of a series of modules that are based on ITIL, and provide the particular configuration that suites the business. Interactive live demos are good for companies looking to develop an ITIL framework, since it offers a full line and complete consulting services regarding ITIL; whether the organization is looking for private or public training.

Some ITIL training centers waste the budget for IT by doing inefficient jobs. An interactive demo helps incorporate the guidelines of ITIL to services and processes that are automated, and can help reduce the cost of operation and improve the relations of the employees that have undergone the live demo. Interactive demos usually offer different categories for various companies like: awareness, assessment of the present status of the organization, designing of the system, organization of the staff, educating the people behind the company of the new concepts and ideas regarding the organization, and lastly, the auditing of finances.

These categories are services that are not necessarily adapted linearly by their nature; these are just some representations of the logical progression of an ITIL framework. It can be gained in the long-term, starting from the adoption of the interactive live demo to the implementation of all the planned applications, and functions of the company for the improvement of its quality and training services.

How to Effectively Use an ITIL Interactive Process Map

Information Technology Infrastructure Library (ITIL) has long defined the best practices in the IT industry. It is an excellent guide on how an organization can go about planning, implementing, maintaining and improving the quality of service that an IT company delivers to its clients and customers. Naturally, each organization has a different set of objectives, but the good thing about ITIL is that the guidelines and framework are not followed to the letter. Instead, they can be defined according to the needs of your organization. One of the best ways for you to have a deeper understanding of the ITIL language is with the use of an ITIL interactive process map.

Here, you will be given a wide array of activity sequences involving the different levels and areas of IT service management. For example, a Service Delivery Manager who is ITIL certified will know what to do when developing service catalogues, establishing contracts, as well as monitoring, reporting and analyzing service levels; all with the help of an ITIL interactive process map. Using this helpful tool, an IT manager can modify existing process models easily, rather than starting from scratch. Also, he can easily document the processes using the ITIL models and document templates to ensure that efficient IT services will be provided to the clients. Finally, with an ITIL interactive process map, you will be given a set of user-friendly ITIL tools and know-how's regarding your projects on IT process management, which all aim to improve your company and your business as a whole.

The Service Management of ITIL

The Information Technology Infrastructure Library is composed of six sets of best standard books. One of the sets is the IT Service Management, which is divided into two areas: the Service Support and the Service Delivery. Even if ITIL consists of many areas, it certainly focuses on the area of IT service management. The two areas mentioned consist of different disciplines that are responsible for the effectiveness of the management of the IT services. There are some questions that can be used as guides to manage the services properly.

- Is the measurement of the IT results based on the outcome of the business?
- Can problems be identified and solved even before it threatens the goal of the business?
- Can the manager control the risks to the business due to changes that may be either planned or unplanned?
- Does the manager have the right control of the processes regarding service management, and can he comply with the requirements?

It must be remembered that businesses today must have a strong foundation to respond to the growing demand for growth, competitive threats, mergers, changes in the market and regulatory compliance. Due to these different demands, IT departments are looking for and developing more ways to meet all the demands, and implement them in a cost-effective and sustainable way.

IT departments turn to the IT service management framework of ITIL for these kinds of processes. However, it must also be remembered that the service management of ITIL is not a solution, but a framework. It only tells the things that should be done, but not the solutions or how to do them. ITIL are sets of standards and best practices.

The Job Description of ITIL

The success or failure of managing the services for ITIL in an organization depends on hiring the best staff and crew in the managerial position. It is essential for any company to have a process of selection for the staff, clarifying all the criteria that meet the company needs. The attributes are generally required for a prospective ITIL job are: communication and interpersonal skills, management skills, knowledge and experience in information technology, and personal skills.

Each discipline that will be needed by the company of a particular staff member requires the uniqueness of the personal attributes, in addition to the ones generally required by the company. These must be identified in the process of selecting, to make sure that the right people are acquired. The steps in the process of selection include the standard application of the prospective staff with an application form to easily compare one from the other.

An interview is also required to obtain the right information about the applicant, their attributes and qualifications, and their experience and knowledge on a particular area. After the interview is evaluation. As the applicant is interviewed, he will be evaluated according to his personality traits, strengths, interpersonal skills, decision-making and leadership traits. The questions to be asked during the interview can help in the evaluation process. The process of selecting the best applicant is time consuming. There are also agencies that can help in the process of recruitment and specialize in the search for a qualified ITIL staff. Hiring with the use of agencies can assist the company by gaining new concepts and ideas, and it is cost-effective in the long run.

The Significant Role of ITIL Management

It is mandatory for a management team to display a high level of commitment and competence to help an organization navigate its way to success. However, in the highly competitive world of business, that may not be enough. Management may also need to find ways to improve the quality of service provided to their customers. The best way to do so is through updating the Information Technology resources of the organization, which is what many industries do nowadays. Through the clear understanding of Information Technology Infrastructure, management can make sure the organization will be able to improve IT-dependent services to customers. Successful application of the technology is further achieved when management is reliant on the Information Technology Infrastructure Library (ITIL) approach.

The basic function of ITIL Management is to manage the Service Support and Service Delivery departments, which are the two key areas of ITIL Management. ITIL Management incorporates an overview of the business into its systems design for the benefit of senior management, so that they can oversee the effective delivery of IT services to customers. Both the positions of Service Support and Service Delivery should be occupied by competent senior managers who hold an accredited ITIL Foundation Certificate, and an ITIL Service Manager Certificate as well.

The ITIL Service Support Manager and the ITIL Service Delivery Manager must also possess five years of training and experience in any of the following areas: IT Service Support, IT Service Delivery, IT Consultancy, IT Project Management and IT Program Management.

They should be highly knowledgeable in ITIL best practices. They must furthermore be able to fully support the integration of ITIL Service Improvement programs within the organization. Lastly, they ought to be able to make the most of all the necessary resources, so that the business can truly benefit from the IT environment they have created.

ITIL Manager's Case Input About ITIL Security Management

First, a word about ITIL Security Management: this is the part of the ITIL manuals that is concerned with the security protocols that are set in place in an information technology system, with emphasis on information security in particular.

It is vital that ITIL Managers get to examine and contribute input about security-related cases that may affect correct establishment and implementation of ITIL Security Management practices within the organization. This is because ITIL Managers are in a position to diagnose exactly what went wrong in the security system of the IT system; or if not, they may be able to accurately describe the events that took place that led to the discovery of the problem. ITIL Managers thus function like information security detectives who will hunt down the cause of breakdown in security so that it will never happen again.

ITIL Security Management derives its importance from the fact that there are stipulations in national and international laws, legally-binding contracts like Service Level Agreements, and both internally and externally-used policies that require the organization to guarantee the security of all information that passes through its portals. Another reason for the importance of ITIL Security Management is that no organization will be able to continue operating if there are severe or even minor breaches in its security protocols.

It should not be thought that ITIL Security Management functions in a vacuum, independent of the other areas of concern in ITIL. Rather, it is interrelated with the other ITIL areas such as: Change Management, Problem Management, Incident Management and Service Desk, Release Management, Configuration

Management, IT Service Continuity Management, Capacity Management, Availability Management, Service Level Management, and of course IT Customer Relationship Management.

Indeed, every organization has to be concerned about security breaches because no customer (regardless of whether that customer is a corporate client or simply a John or Jane Doe) will stand for his data being compromised by poor security systems in the IT system of the organization.

Peep Into an ITIL Manager's Certificate Exam Blog

The ITIL manager's certificate exam is a serious course, which is intended to help IT service managers to be aware of the need to have in-depth knowledge, and gain more practical understanding in ITIL processes, whether they are organizational or process-oriented. Practical oriented courses leading one to be trained in the ITIL manager's certificate include activities such as role-playing and case studies, which both aim to test and improve the managerial skills of the participants.

One of the main objectives to be born in mind when training a service manager is to provide the necessary practical information and skills in planning, management, implementation and improvement of ITIL service support and service delivery processes. Moreover, there are other key objectives in training a service manager, which are: understanding the foundation of all the best ITIL practices; being aware of the importance of IT service management; being able to do impact analysis; determining organizational improvement; and preparation for future certifications.

Part of the certification process consists of an in-course assessment. Before you may obtain a manager's certificate in IT service management, the in-course assessment must have satisfactory results. Assessment ensures the candidate possesses the skills that are necessary for him to function as a manager in IT organization, or perhaps as a consultant.

Having an ITIL foundation certificate under your belt, and possessing good writing and speaking skill, as well as being blessed with two or more years of experience as a professional manager or consultant in the IT management field are all necessary prerequisites for one planning on taking the managerial certificate.

The main objective of these managerial certificate exams are for exam takers to obtain knowledge in managing, recording and improving ITIL processes; be able to describe IT service management processes; be able to implement changing processes; and of course having adequate verbal and writing skills to permit creation of coherent reports, memos and project plans. All these are considered important for one to be able to imbibe the important skills that are required to become a successful service manager.

Use ITIL Mock Test to Soar Your Way Through the IT Industry

No matter which type of industry your business is in, there is a need to keep up with the latest technology to be able to update and improve the products or services that your company offers. ITIL (Information Technology Infrastructure Library) is basically a set of "definitions" on how an IT company can consistently deliver quality technological services. Here, a set of best practices is implemented using techniques, methods, rewards and activities which all aim to improve IT management.

Now, if you are part of the ever-changing IT industry, there is a need for you to pass the ITIL Foundation Exam. This is sometimes a requirement or a preference of companies prior to hiring qualified candidates. There are three tests that you can take to be ITIL certified: the ITIL Foundation Exam, the ITIL V2 Foundation Exam and the ITIL V3 Foundation Exam. To prepare yourself for taking any of them, you can use the ITIL mock tests available over the Internet. How can they prepare you? First, you will have an idea of the types of questions that you can expect, especially if it is your first go at an ITIL Foundation exam. Make sure that the set of ITIL mock tests that you take is related to the foundation's exam syllabus. Finally, try to spread your knowledge over every subject under the ITIL library framework; so that when you encounter any type of question, even during an ITIL mock test, you will not be completely stumped. An ITIL mock test will definitely be your best guide in passing the exam and getting that all-important ITIL certification.

Downloadable ITIL PDF Training Materials

If you would like to study for the ITIL Foundation Certification exam, you can make use of downloadable ITIL PDF training materials available on the Internet. ITIL stands for Information Technology Infrastructure Library, and is a set of frameworks and guidelines involving the best practices, approach, methods and processes so that an Information Technology company can deliver high-quality service to its clients. The ITIL Foundation Certification exam has 40 questions, and the examinee needs at least 65% correct to pass. For those who would like to attain a higher level of knowledge when it comes to ITIL frameworks, principles and guidelines, they can take the ITIL Version 2 or Version 3 examination. When you have an ITIL certification, you are qualified to implement service management techniques within your organization, and you can take part in service support functions for the improvement of your business as a whole.

To assist you while studying for any of the ITIL certification exams, you can use any of the downloadable ITIL PDF training materials, which are easily accessible over the Internet. If you are just starting out with your studies for the ITIL Foundation Certification exam, you can read though a PDF file of the ITIL Essential Study Guides. The website www.theartofservice.com offers a lot of PDF files for those who would like to learn more about ITIL which are entitled: "ITIL V2 Process Model", "Key Differences between ITIL V2 and V3", "IT SMF ITIL V3 Roadshow Presentation", and finally, PDF files that include a glossary of terms for ITIL Versions 2 and 3. These downloadable files will definitely help you prepare for your ITIL certification exams.

Be ITIL Certified, Take Advantage of ITIL Practice Exams

Do you remember when you were in college and you used to take mock exams or practice tests with your study group while preparing for your midterms or finals? Now that you are an IT professional, you can still take advantage of practice exams as you find ways to advance your knowledge and career in the IT technology industry. One of the exams that you can get is the Information Technology Infrastructure Library examination for you to be ITIL certified. ITIL is basically a definition of the best practices, processes and methods used in the IT services industry, and it is widely known and used by companies worldwide. While studying for the ITIL Foundation Certification exam, you can take practice tests to have an idea of how the real examinations will go. You can either take the basic ITIL Foundation Certification exam, or the ITIL Version 2 or Version 3 certification for those who would like to have an advanced knowledge of ITIL processes.

You can easily go online and look for free ITIL practice exams to test the field. With these practice exams, you will know which types of questions might appear on the ITIL exam syllabus. Once you have gained enough knowledge of the principles, frameworks, guidelines and know-how's under the ITIL Foundation Certification exam, you can take ITIL practice exams to see how much more you need to study. By checking your knowledge, you can easily reach the 65% passing mark, and be one step away from getting your ITIL Foundation Certification.

What Should I Do To Become an ITIL Practitioner?

Any person practicing any particular profession is automatically called a practitioner. An ITIL Practitioner is an IT professional who knows how to apply the ITIL technology, and is a holder of the ITIL Practitioner Certificate. They are the people who have chosen a career in the very challenging field of Information Technology, which is the cornerstone of the highly automated modern business world.

Who are these IT Practitioners? They are the professionals who participate in the management, organization, and optimization of the operations in an IT service organization. The IT Practitioners are equipped with the skills for planning, monitoring, reporting and optimizing. These skills are used to support the processes of Release and Control, or Support and Restore. An ITIL Foundation Certificate is the prerequisite to obtaining the next level certificate, which is the ITIL Practitioner Certificate. The ITIL Certification Management Board (ICMB) is the agency that releases the certifications while EXIN and ISEB are the globally-recognized, independent IT examination providers. The examination providers guarantee the quality of the IT Practitioners by means of the independent testing certification.

Before any IT professional can call himself an ITIL Practitioner, he should already have gone through several training courses and learned situations in the field of ITIL. If one is confident enough to call himself an ITIL Practitioner, it is only natural for customers to seek precision from his work.

An ITIL Practitioner has to contend daily with the advancements in technology. It is therefore imperative for an ITIL Practitioner to continue the process of learning every day, and to get abreast with the latest advances and/or innovations in the business. The Internet itself is flooded with information regarding the latest changes in the IT world. The fast-paced world of IT may leave you behind if you exert little to no effort to keep up. You cannot "rest on your laurels," so to speak.

An Introduction to Prince 2

PRINCE is the shorthand term for Projects In Controlled Environments, a process-based system applied for useful project management. PRINCE 2, however, is an actual standard that is extensively used by the UK government, and which is also broadly used by those in the private sectors, both within the UK and abroad.

PRINCE 2 is a method in a public domain, and can offer non-proprietary best practices for guiding project management. It is also a registered trademark of the OGC (Office of Government Commerce) of the UK government.

What are the features of PRINCE 2?

The main concerns of PRINCE 2 are to focus on business justification; emphasizing a team definition in organizing the structure used for project management, maintaining a product-based approach in planning, using a definite cycle, definition of possible problems, dividing projects into a controllable and manageable sequence, and having the capacity to be flexible in applying an appropriate level for a project.

Bringing to the fore all the PRINCE 2 characteristics is known to be very effective in saving time and money because of successful project deliveries.

PRINCE was established back in 1989 by the Central Computer and Telecommunications Agency (CCTA.), now called the OGC. It was originally based on PROMPT, a method of project management that was created by Simpact System Ltd. It was then adopted by CCTA in 1979 to be used in all projects involving government information systems.

PRINCE was then launched in 1989 to take the place of PROMPT immediately throughout all government projects. It has remained in the public domain and is copyrighted.

PRINCE 2 was then published in 1996, and is known to contribute to the systems of around 150 European organizations. PRINCE 2 followed suit in the UK, and has now become one of the most widely used project management methods.

Why ITIL Problem Management is Valuable to Organizations

ITIL problem management was designed so decision-makers can know why incidents occur. Incidents that are considered would be those that pose a minor threat, a great risk or may create a highly negative situation. The ITIL problem management process focuses on "heavy hitters" that may reoccur often, and have significant impact on the organization. However, it is not guaranteed that the organization members will find the origin of the incidents all the time, or that they can permanently restore systems back to normal after every incident.

Success is measured in terms of how frequently problems have been recognized and removed from the existing IT environment, as well as categorization of resolved cases that are considered closed files.

Incidents can be accidental outcomes of an operation in a sequential system. These incidents can interrupt the services that the customer is expecting to receive. Incidents are usually reported to the service desk first, which follows-up with a report about the incident. This first step is dubbed "incident occurrence."

The second step would be assessment of the incident. An incident that was never explained, and that later escalated into a far bigger problem is of special concern. If the cause is unknown, the incident is then called a "problem."

Third is the review of the features of the problem. Here it is important to determine the origin of the problem. As soon as the problem is conclusively proven to exist, it is then renamed as a "known error."

The whole process involves assessment of the known error, determining its indicators, matching it with existing documented problems, and (if there is a match) then referencing to the previously-solved error. It then becomes a simple matter to apply the previously-used solution. On the other hand, if the known error was not solved in the past, then a new record must be created to prevent the error from cropping up again once a similar incident happens. This is dubbed "addressing the error," which is the fourth and last step.

The incidents, problems and known errors may show where problems that were unexpected were encountered during operation of the information system. We thus see that minimizing a debilitating crash is the most important aim of problem management.

The Importance of ITIL Problem Management Procedures

ITIL problem management procedures are used by organizations to try to minimize the impact of incidents on business, caused by errors within the IT infrastructure. Problem management procedure works when the ITIL personnel seek out incident types that frequently crop up. These are then solved through identification of the original cause so that these incidents do not recur anymore. Problem management works first through detection and then by removal of what has caused the failure.

Implementation of Problem Management

In problem management, a good course of action should be both reactive and proactive. Any effective problem management procedure must be fully equipped with the features of both Reactive and Proactive Problem Management.

In Reactive Problem Management, one is concerned with solving problems as a reaction to not just one, but multiple incidents. Proactive Problem Management concentrates more on identifying then solving errors and problems before they can occur.

We can also label the procedure as being part of Reactive Problem Management if it provides permanent fixes to known errors. Another key to Reactive Problem Management is its ability to identify and configure an immediate response to the cause of the event.

Every IT manager would like to know what the future holds for plans to work out perfectly. But sadly, even with organized positive activity, a cycle of more incidents may still happen. The good part is that most incidents can be controlled with use of Proactive Problem Management and its predictive analysis tools.

You know that Proactive Problem Management works if it can prevent incident recurrence, predict service failure, provide a known-error database, respond to time modules, collect data efficiently and easily, perform advance analysis, get broad and deep management perspectives, rapidly detect and anticipate impending problems, manage IT infrastructure within a service context, adapt easily by use of unique infrastructure, and maintain a diagnostic console to improve administrator productivity.

Getting to Know the Different ITIL processes

ITIL service support processes are divided into six major areas of concern, namely: service desk or help desk, incident management, problem management, configuration management, change management, and release management.

The help desk or service desk is a solitary point of focus for all IT services made for clients, responsible for reporting problems or requests for services. Service desk processes consist of tracking and escalating procedures. Moreover, the service desk is also in charge of distributing information to organizations with regards to plans and stages, and also the implementation of change impacts within service production.

Incident management focuses on restoring services following an incident. Incident management basically is a reactive process that provides diagnostic guidance and tends to react as quickly as possible to restore service.

Problem management focuses on identifying the ways preventive measures become necessary, and the cause of service-related issues. It processes reactive responses triggered by incidents and identifies them to prevent future occurrence.

Configuration management guides staff in the collection and archiving of reports about individual infrastructure component specifications. The database of configuration management is a single repository. It contains information with regards to the relationship and dependencies among the components of an infrastructure.

Change management manages the changes that are newly introduced into the IT infrastructure. Change management assesses risks wrought by the changes. Its goal is to identify application codes, detect performance defects and intercept problems before customers are affected by them. Change management is successful if it causes no unwanted effects on the business unit or the customers.

And last, release management is closely interrelated with change management. It addresses large-scale changes within the environment such as reinstalling a new form of database for managing the system, or a widespread change in the entire business application.

The Impact of Using an ITIL Process Mapping Demo

Process mapping provides the company with effective flow-charts that give clear meaning to the individual operation of each department. It is an overview of how things are done in the business organization, and how its services are presented and delivered to the customers. It is also expected to provide the business with ways to map and process the area that needs improvement in efficiency, reducing costs and increasing ROI. Process mapping optimizes IT-dependent business processes.

ITIL Process Mapping Demo must provide information on how the IT company can help the business gain dramatic improvements utilizing ITIL process mapping.

The Demo must successfully sell decision-makers on how valuable process mapping can be to the business, in ways such as:

- Achievement of goals: To provide the business with a specific program of activities through process mapping.
- A snapshot of the business operation: To provide the company a view of how actual things are done in the operation of the business. From manufacturing, maybe, up to how the finish product is delivered to the customers.
- Cross departmental view of the organization: To let the company see through the eyes of the customer to improve customer satisfaction.
- Give greater adaptability to IT operations: Provide a fast solution to standardization of the organization. A

user-friendly process mapping that guarantees easy to incorporate programs (compared to the one currently utilized). Guarantee successful process mapping and improvement within the company and even down to the satisfied customers.

ITIL process mapping must be able to present a top level perspective of the entire organization, with all its departments and projects considered as well. The demo must be able to satisfy the doubts and questions of the decision-makers. It must also achieve the ITIL process mapping demo objective of being able to close a registration or a contract.

Features of an ITIL Sample Test

ITIL exam takers are often provided with sample test questionnaires to prepare them for the real examination. There are sample exam questionnaires based on actual ITIL papers so that you can experience the real thing.

Each sample test consists of 40 questions. All questions provide you with four choices to choose as answers, with only one possible correct answer. You have to answer all of the questions within an hour and get a passing grade of at least 26 right answers.

Sample test questions:

Basically, the test questions you will be provided with all have a relationship to ITIL. It includes questions such as: How can you best describe the key characteristics of Service Desk Staff? For what purpose is this particular ITIL process responsible for? What kind of information does configuration management provide for management of an organization? There are many possible answers given in a range of choices per question, but the test taker must only choose one answer per question, which would be the best answer as far as he is concerned.

Sample questions such as these are provided by the ITIL foundations to test the skills of exam takers and help them prepare for the actual exam. The sample test helps exam takers train for the disciplines of configuration management, service desk management, incident management, problem management, change management, release management, SLM, financial management, availability management, capacity management, ITSCM and other subjects as well. This is very useful to the test taker who wants to get the most comprehensive knowledge of ITIL he can.

Though a sample test may include only some questions similar to those in the real exam, it can still adequately prepare the test taker to be at his best, and be able to perform well during the actual exam.

Free ITIL Sample Tests Available Online

Any student who is about to take an exam is anxious to know what the test questions are about. Those who take board exams and bar exams are no different from the average person in that respect. It is a welcome relief then that review schools offer pre-testing and other tips helpful for passing an exam. ITIL schools also offer copies of an ITIL Sample Test and trial testing. The sample test is available free on line. The actual exam contains 40 questions which are supposed to be answered within 60 minutes. The exam is in the form of multiple choices with a passing score of 26 out of 40.

What is the use of going through a sample test? Well, we know that our brain has more storage capacity than that of any computer, and it is capable of storing volume upon volume of information. Therefore, the lessons we have learned before are stored up in our brain. However, just like computers, there are times when we need to click on the refresh button to activate some files. This is why we use reviews and sample tests.

A Free ITIL Sample Test is like taking the actual exam (minus the stress). Familiarity with the type of questions to be given gives the person preparing for the exam added confidence in taking the actual exams. There have been actual cases wherein the test examinee blacks out and therefore fails the exams. To avoid situations such as that, it is best to open an ITIL sample test free on line. Take several of them, because using them will make taking the real exam less stressful, and fill you with confidence.

Features of Any Standard ITIL Service Delivery Case

ITIL service delivery is an IT management fundamental. Service delivery is concerned specifically with the ability of the service provider to supply the services offered to the client organization. Particularly, it deals with the required elements in providing the service like continuity, security, availability, and financial capacity; as well as the necessity of IT transportation capacity.

Here is a brief summary of the main aspects of the methods for service delivery defined by ITIL standards:

The first part is grouped into three classifications: The Customers who are the party responsible for contracting IT services and listing down the IT projects given to the right service provider account. The Users, the people who are responsible for using the IT services in question, so they can function in their assigned tasks within their employer organization. The Organization, this is the IT group which is said to be the client for the IT services provided by the service provider.

The second part in service delivery involves service level management. This means defining the IT services given as formally stated in the service level agreements, and identifying operations dealing with what the customers need, and computing the costs. The people tasked with service level management are also responsible for making reports based on the quality of service.

The third part is called CMDB (or configuration management database), which deals with the detailed information about system configuration, like hardware and software. It also tackles the interrelationship between the different configurations of these items.

The fourth part is devoted to availability management, which is basically about making sure that the IT service provider can always be available and reliable with IT services properly maintained to ensure good service.

The fifth part, which is based on capacity management, will require staff to draw up capacity plans, monitor IT performance, and even simulate capacity requirements. It is responsible for computing supply since the staff has to predict what is needed.

The sixth part lists the area of financial management, where its people are responsible for measuring the financial cost of the service and tagging the preferred service provider who can offer a reasonable price.

The last part gives information about IT Service Continuity Management that evaluates, and draws up contingency plans, so that the service provider can assure the rapid recovery of the service when disastrous and severe faults in the IT infrastructure rear their ugly head.

Recognizing the Need for ITIL Services

Customers always seem to want the latest advances in IT, yet have to contend with rigid budgets. An IT-dependent customer has to work light, but also work smart. According to the ITIL standard, to improve the effectiveness and efficiency of your IT system, you will need to implement Service Level Management or SLM.

A customer who is aware of the six ITIL service supports will be able to adopt IT service so that his IT tools can function at their best. First, there is configuration management, which relies on the CMDB or Configuration Management Database to control and manage infrastructure information. The second area is problem management, which relies on a combination of active and proactive analysis to allow automatic problem identification. There is also incident management, which permits definition of incident workflows that functions by combining states and transitions with defined and configurable business processes. Change management, on the other hand, allows management of changes in a coordinated fashion that will be aligned with the documented management procedures. Fifth is the service or help desk, which attempts to ensure that ITIL practices rely on the best known responses to incidents and fixes them within the time limit. Lastly, release management allows for all conclusions about the causes and proposed solutions of the incidents to be made.

ITIL is essential since it attempts to improve IT service to the point that it functions in an effective and efficient manner, resulting in good quality of service on the whole.

Some of the known IT service best practices would be: continuous improvement of IT service delivery; reduction of costs through the process of improvement; producing a higher level of efficiency; reduction of risks inherent to the business through rapid delivery of consistent and recoverable services; improved communication to create better working relationships within IT and business organizations; and fostering the ability to succeed in business (among many others).

Though comprehensive IT management can be difficult to achieve, organizations can succeed in implementing ITIL processes if they can figure out the complexities that form part and parcel of it. IT management decision-makers must accept the fact that there is no easy way or quick fixes to solve a problem; they have to pursue problem resolution one step at a time to iron out problems completely.

How ITIL Software Asset Management Can Benefit You

The challenge in Asset Management and Configuration lies with the delivery of quality IT services that both client and service provider can agree upon, particularly with regards to the service levels. At the same time, Asset Management and Configuration efforts should help the client organization be able to adapt to changes within the operating environment of its business. Software asset management requires that the client organization be able to implement ways to secure the maximum value out of IT production and services so that in the end, the business can ensure the highest possible return of investment in the infrastructure.

To balance these priorities, there is a need for effective asset management and configuration management software that is founded on a solid base. This helps the client to be sure that it is getting the best service from its outsourced IT service support and delivery. Having a best-practices base for the Asset Management and Configuration Management software will allow successful implementation of said functions.

Asset management software provides real-time insight that will help you to take control of tracking capability, such as calculating and knowing the assets you currently have, the worth of all of the assets, where they are located, how effective they are in supporting your business, and how well they are presently working. Many organizations are willing to invest a lot in software whether for internal or external usage.

Some of the benefits brought about by asset management are:

- the supply of accurate information for all IT configuration items that can support the service delivery and the support process;
- provision of trend and impact analysis information in change management and problem management;
- improvement in IT security featuring an advantageous configuration in item control;
- an increase in customer satisfaction;
- improvement in financial planning through clear identification of all the assets and all related associations;
- improved software license management; and
- increased confidence in IT service management and the IT system being used.

ITIL Templates, the Key to Effective IT Service Management

What are ITIL templates? Basically, these are your easy-to-understand references when it comes to Information Technology Infrastructure Library implementation. If your organization is complying with the ITIL guidelines, then you will find that ITIL templates to be beneficial. First, the people who will benefit from using ITIL templates include the following: employees who are dealing with the creation and customization of your company's Service Level Agreement; those who are in charge of service catalogs; and the managers who are implementing any changes in the company's business processes.

The Internet is your best source for ITIL templates. When you go to a website which has an entire list of ITIL templates, you can look for ones under different categories like configuration management, incident management, change management, service level management, service desk, IT financial management and a lot more. If you choose "Configuration Management," for example, you will see a list of questions to ask your company's management before implementing any changes in your business process. If you choose "Change Management," there may be a checklist or a ready-made flow chart that you can follow. However, you need to remember that ready-made ITIL templates need to be analyzed to determine whether they will achieve the same goals that you have as a company. As long as you keep in mind that ITIL templates need to be revised to fit your needs, then you can definitely make use of them in order to save time, energy and company resources while effectively implementing ITIL standards.

Your Complete ITIL Tips Guide

No matter how small or big your company is, Information Technology plays a big role in the application and implementation of the services provided to your clients and customers. ITIL (Information Technology Infrastructure Library) is an across-the-board standard that you can use to ensure your company's successful operation on a day-to-day basis. Take a look at the following ITIL tips guide for organizations that are implementing the Information Technology Infrastructure Library: First, do not consider the ITIL frameworks and guidelines as a strict rulebook. In fact, just the opposite is true because you can use the models in such a way that it will be suitable to meet your company's goals and objectives.

Prior to the implementation of ITIL principles in your organization, make sure that you have the complete backing of the higher-ups in management and your company's IT department. Next, have a brainstorming session with the experts and look at which business processes need to be changed immediately. As you start with the ITIL implementation on your business processes, monitor the progress made so that you can work out the kinks in the plan at the earliest time possible. Communication among all departments is also crucial if you want to see and experience the benefits of ITIL implementation within your company. Generally, what you need to do is make each member or division in the company understand how the ITIL implementation will impact the business as a whole. With ITIL implementation, you can slowly but surely work your way toward your company's success and ensure the full satisfaction of your clients in the IT industry.

Choosing the Right ITIL Training Center

There are quite a number of ITIL Training Centers that offer their services in the market today. Browse through the Internet and you will find a lot that make similar claims. But your ultimate purpose as an IT professional is to advance your career and get the Certificates you need after the training. This means that you need to pass the exam and take hold of that prized certificate, and that entails enrolling with the right ITIL training center.

When choosing the right ITIL training center, you must consider some things that a quality center must have.

First and foremost, the center must be accredited by the government (of the country you work in) to give exams and issue certificates.

The ITIL Training Center, as well as their instructors, must have enough experience in the trade or course they handle. You would feel bad if your instructor demonstrated inferior knowledge compared to you, who is not yet a professional. Forthright training providers should make available to students the educational and professional background of their instructors before students even enroll.

Usually, this kind of training involves payment of substantial tuition fees. You should treat this as a career investment, so be meticulous in your choice. Check the amount of fees they charge, are they within industry standards? Just because you believe you are guaranteed to receive good pay after you have gotten your certificate does not mean you should just pay any fee amount.

Your training provider must have specialized in the kind of training you are considering. Since ITIL requires technical training that meets globally accepted standards, your provider must show some international accreditation. International certification standards for ITIL are a mandatory requirement all training providers have to meet.

The training center must also have a laboratory, complete with a full range of ITIL books. Review helps a lot, so mock exams must be included in their curriculum.

Having good training will give you that necessary edge so that you can pass the exams. You will then be able to achieve your objective of getting the certificate or certificates you need in the future.

Does an ITIL Career Pay a Good Wage?

The major concerns you should have in choosing a career path would be your interests and your abilities. Getting into a career that does not interest you and does not match your abilities is a futile move. The other factors that can help a career-seeker decide on how to direct their career path are: the availability of good job opportunities, the global acceptance of such an occupation, and the potential income and benefits one can get from the profession. These factors are all satisfied in the Information Technology profession.

An IT profession may become a more rewarding career if you simply keep adding a few more training courses and studies to your "cap." Being globally accepted and utilized, an IT career can bring you a prosperous future and long-lasting employment prospects. IT is well accepted as a basic tool in any industry and/or occupation, and could therefore be rated as a must for any organization to possess as a resource. The practical question though is: does it pay well?

A Global Knowledge market organization listed the ITIL Managers Certificate as being fifth in the top ten lists of the ten highest-paying certifications one can get in the technology industry. The average annual salary of an ITIL Manager Certificate was listed at $94,000.00. Those with an ITIL Practitioners Certificate are believed to earn an average annual income of $87,917.00. People who choose to pursue Information Technology careers can expect an average annual income of $112,088.00 (being the highest) and $78,579 (the base) as of June 2007.

You may find the figures encouraging and may now decide to take the plunge into an IT career (and may even get into the ITIL field as well). However, you should keep in mind that those figures are currently being earned by those IT professionals who are deeply focused on their careers. If you wish to get the maximum benefits, such as great wages from an IT career, you should remember this: set a career goal then stick to it. This means being very focused on your work so that you can earn the rewards.

IT Service Management and ITIL - Working Together Toward Total Customer Satisfaction

Customer satisfaction is one of the main goals, if not the top priority of a service-oriented company. If customers are happy with the service being provided, then it also means continued patronage, and a key determinant in improving the quality of provisioned service within an imposed cost constraint. In information technology, an IT service concept also focuses on what the consumer receives, and this is where Information Technology Service Management (ITSM) fits within the organization.

IT Service Management focuses on managing the IT components so as to provide the best quality service to customers in the most cost-effective and efficient way. Like Information Technology Infrastructure Library (ITIL), ITSM involves embracing well-defined best practices that organizations should adopt. The concept of ITSM is at the heart of ITIL and is generally divided into two main areas: Service Delivery and Service Support.

Service Delivery consists of all the planning, development and delivery of quality IT services and in the long run, involves the processes of finding ways to improve the quality of service delivered. The five disciplines under Service Delivery are: Service Level Management, Capacity Management, Contingency Planning, Availability Management and IT Financial Management. On the other hand, Service Support is a discipline that focuses on the users of the ICT services, in which they get involved in the process whenever they ask for changes or updates in the service, have difficulties accessing the service, or have queries about the service. The six Service Support disciplines are: Configuration Management, Problem Management, Incident Management, Change Management, Service Help Desk and Release Management.

Microsoft and ITIL

The Microsoft Company has been involved in the community of ITIL for years. Both are adapting the contents of ITIL and contribute to the latest, expanded and updated documentation of Microsoft. ITIL offers a wide range of guidance documents that feature the service delivery IT management and support, including the essential parts of the IT infrastructure. Safety and security of the organization and the management of all its applications are the other features of the document. ITIL helps in promoting the application of descriptive guidance to attain improvement in the different areas of service management with continuity.

Microsoft has the Microsoft Operations Framework (MOF) as a collection of best practices, models and principles that is built under the IT Infrastructure Library (ITIL). The approach used by MOF is prescriptive and promotes the continuous improvement of the capabilities of IT service management using the process-driven tools. This is in contrast to the approach of ITIL, which is descriptive. To further discuss the Microsoft Operations Framework, the framework is the one making the necessary adjustments for the ever changing needs of any business. It optimizes all the processes for the increase in efficiency.

The principle of ITIL, when applied to the Microsoft technology, provides the foundation in helping different IT organizations to meet all the challenges that may be encountered, and assist in their goal for the continual improvement of the organization. It can give guidance to the operation and will enable the business to attain the critical missions of their systems with the high reliability and availability of the Microsoft products and its technologies.

Carrying Out a Normal Change in ITIL

Many decision-makers may not be aware of the two main objectives of change management in ITIL. The first is to improve the effectiveness and efficiency of daily operations while the second is to limit change-related incidents.

Most of the time, the first objective is what ITIL change management implementers often forget. This results in a change management effort that becomes bureaucratic, impossible to manage and unrealistic as far as how the implementation staff perceives it.

ITIL can definitely improve the effectiveness and efficiency of the preferred IT solutions, and make the IT staff feel empowered, but it requires the use of correctly standardized changes for that to be realized. Correct implementation of ITIL can be described as being commonly implemented throughout the organization, follows an established path in the infrastructure, and pursues conventional solutions based on set or specified requirements.

There are six steps to help in implementation of standard changes that can ensure it will function properly. These are the creation of a process to authorize standard changes, the creation of a request for change (or RFC), the involvement of a change advisory board (or CAB), the creation of a formal process for the identification, the definition, and the implementation of processes for managing these standardized or normal changes.

Candidates for standard changes should be identified to help in implementation of would-be changes. A SOP (or standard operating procedure) needs to be documented, since it will form the skeleton of the standard changes. The SOP will help define how, when, where, how and for whom any standard changes should be initiated.

After establishing this SOP, decision-makers must review it to see how the organization may perform the task step by step. This also means even the lowest level of IT staff affected must be covered so that they can perform tasks efficiently.

The process of training, testing and releasing will help in communicating the need for and the steps in implementation of the standard changes. Then the SOP will be placed under change management control.

Lastly, managing, monitoring, auditing and reporting come into play. It then becomes necessary to further review the success of the SOP, and the standard change process to make sure that all that was needed to be done was done in an appropriate fashion.

ITIL in PDF - ITIL Documents Made Accessible Online

When searching for web content using the browser's search engine, most of the search results listed are on PDF. When the link is clicked, another window will then appear and the PDF file is displayed as if its contents are scanned or embedded. PDF stands for Portable Document Format, an extension file created by Adobe Systems in the year 1993. The latest version is PDF 1.7, supported by the Adobe Reader version 8.0. PDF files combine three technologies:

- a sub-set of the Post-script page description programming language used for generating the layout and graphics;
- a font-embedding / replacement system used to allow fonts to travel with the documents; and
- a structured storage system to bundle these elements with data compression when appropriate.

Because of these technologies, PDF is widely used nowadays, even in the dissemination of information about ITIL (the Information Technology Infrastructure Library). Since there is a need to acquire training and pass the certification examination to become an ITIL professional, there are a lot of review materials, resource articles and practice papers that come in PDF and can be downloaded online. They can also serve as an easy reference to know the basics of ITIL, if you are considering getting a certification exam in the future. Not only that, ITIL PDF files are also a means of enhancing your ITIL skills, and thus prepare you to have a working knowledge and sound competence as an IT professional. Find an ITIL PDF toolkit and discover ITIL today.

Ways of Getting Badly-Needed ITIL Tutorial

You have probably heard of the Information Technology Infrastructure Library (or ITIL), and may even have been served by an IT company using ITIL. You felt the need to learn more about ITIL, since your company is now ITIL Certified. You are now looking for ways to squeeze into your schedule the necessary time to study about or get a tutorial for ITIL. You searched through the web and found several companies offering tutorial ITIL. Now you know you can either get it by attending a regular class or participating in a tutorial online. What probably pops into your mind next is the question of which is the best school to get a tutorial ITIL from.

The following may guide you in choosing the best company offering tutorial ITIL to the public:

Choose a reputable company or school. Getting word-of-mouth referrals from those who have already attended and have passed the exams for the ITIL Foundation Certificate is a good way to start.

Narrow down the list. Check to see if the company you are eyeing presents a tutorial that is friendly to beginners. Not everyone has a strong IT background. However, almost everyone desires to at least understand ITIL terminologies, if not to actually become very IT literate.

The company should provide tools for learning which are informative but easy to understand. Study materials may include: Powerpoint presentations; live demonstrations; study guides; review exercises; interactive laboratories; and authorized practice exams.

You will know a good tutorial ITIL by the number of successful students it has produced. Check on their achievers since any school would be proud to talk about them.

Remember though that, no matter how good the tutorial ITIL is, nothing can motivate you to learn in order to succeed. It always begins with the individual first.

What is ITIL?

ITIL simply means Information Technology Infrastructure Library. It helps deliver high quality information technology services. ITIL provides a broad set of management procedures that are designed to support businesses in attaining financial value from IT. It is a globally renowned compilation of best practices for IT operations. Originated from Central Computer and Telecommunications Agency (CCTA) in the United Kingdom, they produced the ITIL in accordance to the increasing number of dependence on IT and achieving the business goals of companies.

Big companies such as Microsoft and Hewlett-Packard are just some of the well-known IT businesses that use ITIL as one of their best practices structures. ITIL is composed of different sets: Service Delivery, Planning to Implement Service Management, Service Support, Applications Management, ICT Infrastructure Management and Business Perspective.

Aside from the texts, which can be bought online, the ITIL products and services also contain training, software tools, user groups, and qualifications like IT Service Management Forum (itSMF). ITIL is a framework that aims to improve and facilitate the distribution of premium IT operations. This procedure has a high quality outline and an extensive collection of management procedures that can support and improve procedures in your business.

These processes are supplier-independent, and they upgrade to offer help in the extensive growth and advancement of IT operations and infrastructure. And as the word "library" implies, the ITIL already has a series of books published that discuss the core of IT management.

Since ITIL was created in the U.K. government in the mid 1980's, it started as a project to record the best practice in Information Technology. Soon after, this structure was approved and accepted. In the early 90's huge organizations, businesses and even government agencies in Europe implemented this framework. Information Technology advances each day. That is why it is important to plan, organize, and upgrade framework, structures and operations.

ITIL Procedure Writing

The need to document ITIL based procedures and applications is very important for the business to comply with the necessary ITIL requirements. There are sets of procedures that are off the shelf, but obtaining them this way might require a higher cost in the long run when it comes to modifying them to fit the particular organization. It would be more practical to write a new set rather than modify an old one. The process of writing ITIL requires writers that are proficient in the field of writing and have experience with writing the different procedures.

The writer must also have an IT background, and knows the principles of ITIL. He must have a good understanding of the various types of information involved so as to create well plan policies and procedures that are aimed at the tasks and people concerned.

He must be able to acquire information, conduct interviews with the owners of the processes, and interview the experts who have the right sources of information. He must also be versatile and have additional skills, like mapping processes, making flow charts, authoring tools, and many more. He must be able to format and edit the documents and lastly, he must have a good knowledge of the different requirements, such as publishing and version control.

The procedures in writing ITIL have a lot of subjects to take into consideration. It must be designed to smoothly merge with the procedures and policy of the company's system. It must also consider customer service. Writing ITIL is a struggle at first, but definitely a very rewarding task in the long run.

Printed in the United States
140665LV00002B/82/A

9 780980 459975